At Home in the Woods

A Stehekin Family History – The Moores and Courtneys

Mike Barnhart

ISBN 978-0-9702153-8-3
Barnhart Photography
PO Box 25
Stehekin, WA 98852
www.barnhartphoto.com

Compiled and written by Mike Barnhart
Edited by Ana Maria Spagna
Design/Layout by Sally Ranzau
Proof Reading by Iris Graville

Photography by: J.R. Moore, Mike Barnhart, Nancy Barnhart,
Moore-Courtney family archives, The Wenatchee World, Chelan
County PUD archives, Robin Kammerling, Howe Sound Mining
Company archives, Laura Reiter.

Cover Photo: Courtney home. ca. 1956
Cover Photo Inset: The Courtney Family at home. ca. 1935
    Left to Right: June, Mamie, Hugh, Ray, Laurence, Curt

Back Cover Photos:
Top: Winter at the Moore Hotel ca. 1893
Middle: Curt Courtney and 1922 Dodge at Stehekin. ca. 1946
Bottom: Stearnwheeler, *The Queen of Chelan* approaches Moore
    Point. ca. 1893

Unloading Ice at Moore Point. ca.1898

DEDICATION

This book is dedicated to my mother, June Courtney Barnhart, who passed away in 2002, as the last surviving member of the original Courtney family. Her love for Stehekin never diminished. She often spoke of the hard winters and how much work it was, helping her mom with all the chores, adding on with; "but we always had fun. It was hard work, but we always had fun." Most every page in her journals started out with a couple of lines about house work and chores, but ended with playing with the animals or going to the landing with her brothers.

After moving to town in 1936, my mother only spent short periods of time at Stehekin. Her favorite childhood place to play was up on the hump, a special place up on one of the benches above the valley floor. Even as an adult, the first thing she did after getting settled on a visit was take a walk up on the hump, then a nostalgic and sometimes emotional walk around the old homestead. She really missed her family and the lifestyle on the farm. It was contagious. Her love of this place inspired me to live here and raise a family, a few yards up the road from the cabin where she was born and grew to adulthood; to explore the same special places she explored. She and I talked about how nice it would be to write a book about our family, so Mom here's to you!

–Mike

Hugh Courtney splitting wood while grandson Tom Courtney looks on. ca. 1957

Acknowledgements

I would like to thank all the people who encouraged me to "keep moving" on this project. I found that sailing into uncharted waters, especially as one gets a little older, can be a daunting task. The desire to write this book started many years ago, even to the point of organizing and writing down the stories as I remembered them, but getting down to the nuts and bolts of actually writing a rough outline and moving ahead didn't start until 2009. With the nudging of my wife Nancy, author Ana Maria Spagna and Sally Ranzau, the person who did the actual layout and printing of the book, the desire evolved into a visual format from which I could build on. As each piece of writing was finished, I'd send it off to Ana Maria for editing and her constructive comments. Living in the valley and understanding the lifestyles and hard work involved, plus her expert talents on journal and memoir writing, made her my obvious choice for editing. I can't think of anyone else who could do the job like Ana Maria. Equally deserving, Sally Ranzau's vast experience and dedication to quality in the book publishing business was another obvious choice. In looking back, I think at least part of the reason I didn't start this project years earlier was because I had yet to meet these two people.

I also want to give special thanks to author and publisher Iris Graville for proofreading and excellent suggestions. Iris lived in Stehekin with her family for a few years and also understands the dynamics of how this community functions.

The other folks I wish to thank are most all of my cousins for helping trigger my memory and getting facts right about our family. Sometimes our stories didn't jibe, but usually after a little discussion, we came pretty close and of course had several good laughs over the craziness of how our family carried on up here. My second cousin, Christina Byrd, also provided many historical photos, documents, letters and other information without which I'd be at a loss; second cousin Maria Byrd Vodden for her detailed notes about her grandmother Dorothy Lotspeich Byrd; Jim Trappe, Hobbie Buckner Morehead, Bucky Buckner Gans, Nancy McMinn at the Wenatchee World, Chelan County PUD, NPS files, University Of Washington Special Collections Library, Holden Village archives, my sister, Mary, and her daughter, Cheryl, for diligent on-line research, and especially my wife, Nancy, for listening to me ramble on for the better part of two years, sharing new things I'd discovered about our family. Nancy also helped with the layout and shooting of the artifact groupings for Part II. The last group of folks I am honored to acknowledge, although posthumously, are my great grandparents the Moores, grandparents Hugh and Mamie Courtney, and my mother and her five siblings. Without their stories, letters, documents and photographs there would be no book. In doing the research for this project, I have come to know these folks in a new way. Their heritage needs to be preserved, and I sincerely hope this book will help keep the stories alive.

TABLE OF CONTENTS

Archie Moore rowing at Moore Point. Photo by his father, J.R. Moore.ca. 1899

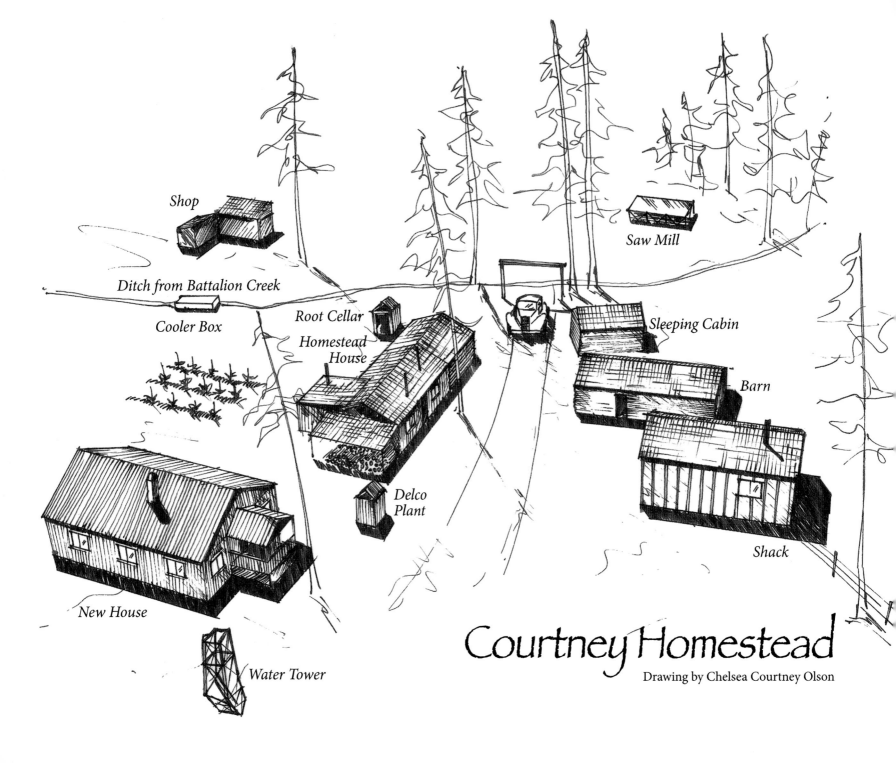

Shop

Ditch from Battalion Creek

Cooler Box

Root Cellar

Homestead
House

Saw Mill

Sleeping Cabin

Barn

Delco
Plant

New House

Shack

Water Tower

Courtney Homestead

Drawing by Chelsea Courtney Olson

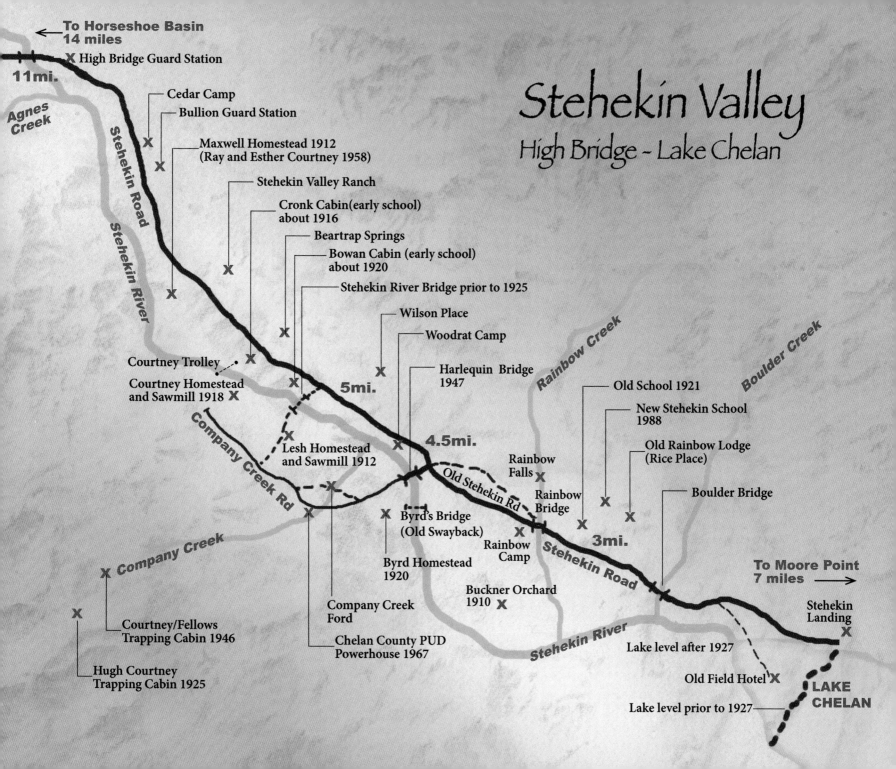

Stehekin Valley
High Bridge - Lake Chelan

← To Horseshoe Basin 14 miles

✗ High Bridge Guard Station

11mi.

Agnes Creek

Stehekin Road

Stehekin River

Cedar Camp

Bullion Guard Station

Maxwell Homestead 1912
(Ray and Esther Courtney 1958)

Stehekin Valley Ranch

Cronk Cabin (early school)
about 1916

Beartrap Springs

Bowan Cabin (early school)
about 1920

Stehekin River Bridge prior to 1925

Wilson Place

Woodrat Camp

Harlequin Bridge
1947

Rainbow Creek

Boulder Creek

Old School 1921

New Stehekin School
1988

Old Rainbow Lodge
(Rice Place)

Boulder Bridge

5mi.

4.5mi.

Courtney Trolley

Courtney Homestead
and Sawmill 1918 ✗

Company Creek Rd

Lesh Homestead
and Sawmill 1912

Old Stehekin Rd

Rainbow
Falls

Rainbow
Bridge

Byrd's Bridge
(Old Swayback)

Company Creek

Byrd Homestead
1920

Rainbow
Camp

Stehekin Road

3mi.

To Moore Point
7 miles →

Stehekin
Landing

Company Creek
Ford

Buckner Orchard
1910 ✗

Stehekin River

Lake level after 1927

Courtney/Fellows
Trapping Cabin 1946

Chelan County PUD
Powerhouse 1967

Hugh Courtney
Trapping Cabin 1925

Old Field Hotel ✗

LAKE
CHELAN

Lake level prior to 1927

THE COURTNEY FAMILY TREE

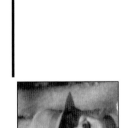

Hugh Laurence Courtney
b. Kansas 12/3/1887
d. Wenatchee, WA 3/10/1964

m. 11/10/1910
Mary Louise (Mamie) Moore

Mary Louise (Mamie) Moore
b. Jamestown, N.Y. 10/4/1886
d. Chelan, WA. 11/3/1950

m.1903
William Felix Lotspeich
B 1873
d. 1962
div. 11/18/1907
===========
m. 11/10/1910
Hugh Laurence Courtney

Laurence Hugh Courtney	**Curtice M. Courtney**	**Katherine June Courtney**	**James Raymond Courtney**	**Harwood Lotspeich**	**Dorothy Mary Lotspeich**
					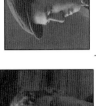

  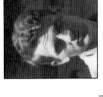       

Laurence Hugh Courtney
b. 6/21/1912
d. 11/4/1986

m. 01/30/1955
Lona Elsie Miller Blankenship
b. 3/07/1916
d. 07/30/2008
===========
son
Laurence Joseph Courtney
b.1956
Janet Louise Kaitis
b.1957
===========
Danielle Sheila-Marie Courtney
b.1987
David Laurence Courtney
b.1990
===========
son
Marvin Douglas Courtney
b.1957
partner
Chella Hiatt
Andrea Lona Courtney
b.1994
===========
m. 1995
Christine Goodwin
div. 2000
Douglas Bryan Courtney
b. 1996
Mariah Patricia Courtney
b. 1998

Curtice M. Courtney
b. 09/05/1915
d. 12/01/2000

m. 1950
Olive Beryl Imus Blankenship
b. 1908
d. 1993
===========

Katherine June Courtney
b. 06/16/1918
d. 11/22/2002

m. 04/12/1940
Kenneth Webster Barnhart
b. 10/01/1917
d. 12/17/2009
===========
daughter
Mary May Barnhart
b. 1941
m. 1958
Clarence Willard Jenkins
b. 1936
d. 1995
===========
Cheryl Anne Jenkins
b. 1960
m. 1981
Scott Bryant
div. 1981
m. 1982
Mark Johnson
b. 1955
div. 1988
===========
James Barry Jenkins
b. 1962
m. 1987
Joyce Weiss
b. 1959
===========
Christopher William Jenkins
b. 1990
Ross Elan Jenkins
b. 1992
===========
Keith Wayne Jenkins
b. 1964
m. 1990
Frances Gatica
b. 1961
Megan Nicole Jenkins
b. 1993

James Raymond Courtney
b. 05/10/1920
d. 08/10/1982

m. 1946
Arlene Thew
b. 8/25/29
div.
d. 5/25/08
===========
son
Bruce Courtney
b. 1948
m.
Martha Wheeler
b.
===========
daughter
Sylvia Courtney
b. 1950
m.
Kerry Larson
b.
===========
Mindy Larsen
b.1970
===========
Jeni
b. 1997
Lindsay Larsen
b. 1978
m.
Marcke
b. 1993
Acasia
b. 2006
===========
m. 1952
Esther Delores Fellows
b. 1930
d. 1991
===========
son
James Oliver Courtney
b. 1953
m. 1980
Irene Marie Strunk
b. 1954
Samantha Delores Courtney
b. 1991
Gorden Fredrick Courtney
b. 1994

Harwood Lotspeich
b. 1904
d. 1968
m. 1943
Hazel Arlena McKamey
b. 1904
d. 1972
===========
daughter
Nedra Lotspeich
b. 1946
d. 2002
m.
Cecil Nard
b. 1919
d. 2002

Dorothy Mary Lotspeich
b. 1905
d. 1984
m. 1924
Charles Franklin Byrd
b. 1888
div. about 1954
d. 1960
===========
son
Robert Lee Byrd
b. 1925
d. 1989
m. 1946
Hilda Marie Scott
b. 1925
d. 2008
===========
Maria May Byrd
b. 1947
m. 1984
Daniel Vodden
b. 1951
Forest Daniel Vodden
b. 1986
===========
Kathleen Carol Byrd
b. 1948
d. 1985
m.
William L. Sullivan
b. 1944
div. 1972
Zen Troy Sullivan
b. 1969
d. 2007
m. 1972
Robert H. Myers
b.
div. 1975
===========
Annette Cecelia Byrd
b. 1950
m. 1971
Erwin Ballard Ellis Jr.
annulled 1974
b. 1945
d. 1992
m. 2003
Kimber K. Kennedy

Genealogy Chart

Harmony Michelle Ellis
b. 1972
partner
Leif Leonard Duncan
b. 1972
separated

Alexandria Aron Michelle Duncan
b. 1991
m.1992
Jeffrey Adam Moore
b. 1968
div.
m. 2011
Shane Ray

Courtney Rose Moore
b. 1992
m. 2001
Justin Barbee

Christina Joy Byrd
b. 1954

daughter
Effie Mae Byrd
b. 1926
m. 1959
Leonard Baillie
b. 1926

Andrew Baillie
b. 1963
d. 1963

daughter
Letha Jeannie Byrd
b. 1929
m.
Harvey R. Ogden
b.
div.

m. 1980
George H. Bell
b. 1923

---

son
Thomas Hugh Courtney
b. 1954
m. 1980
Elizebeth Jane Browder
b. 1957

Michael James Barnhart
b. 1944
m.1969
Karen Elizabeth Friedlander
b. 1952
div. 1975

Chelsea Marie Courtney
b. 1983
m. 2008
J.B. Olsen
b. 1982

Tania Lee Barnhart
b. 1971
Partner
Kent Grasser
b. 1956

Reed Thomas Courtney
b. 1986
m. 2006
Jennifer Sanders

Danita May Grasser
b.1993

Kylan Bree Courtney
b. 2011

Partner
Lawrence W. Kuehne
b. 1956

Warren James Courtney
b. 1997

Tyler Michael Barnhart
b. 1995

Simon Lee Courtney
b. 1999

---

son
Gorden Gene Courtney
b. 1955
d. 1971

m. 1996
Jeffrey Ball
b. 1971
div. 1999

Aiyana June Ball
b. 1997

---

son
Cragg Douglas Courtney
b. 1958
m.1989
Roberta Helen Breeze
b. 1962

Partner
Shane Innes
b. 1956

Victoria K. Barnhart- Innes
b. 2002

Quinlan Breeze Courtney
b. 1992

Clancy Rae Courtney
b. 1994

Neil Douglas Barnhart
b. 1972
d. 1972

---

son
Mark Lewis Courtney
b. 1959
m. 1981
Monica Miller Courtney
b. 1959

Michael James Barnhart Jr.
b. 1974
m. 1993
Jenny Ritter
b. 1974
div. 2008

Jacob Ray Courtney
b.1982
m. 2006
Dawn Parks
b. 1986

Austin James Barnhart
b. 1994

James Raymond Courtney
b. 2008

Shauna Jenée Barnhart
b. 1996

Jessica Cheyenne Barnhart
b. 2001

McKenna Joy Courtney
b. 2010

Ellie Jo Courtney
b. 2011

Partner
Dawn Borsch
b. 1968

Mistaya Mary Courtney
b. 1985

E'ren Rain Borsch Barnhart
b. 2006

---

son
Clifford Garfield Courtney
b. 1961
m. 1987
Kerry Bigelow
b. 1953

m. 2011
Marhya Misner
b. 1979

Logan James Courtney
b. 1989

m. 1978
Nancy Caldwell Apthorp
b. 1952

Owen Christopher Barnhart
b. 1980

m. 2010
Corianne Bowman

Roger Laurence Barnhart
b. 1987

Colter Curtis Courtney
b. 1991

m. 2008
Brooke Reynolds
b. 1987

---

daughter
Peggy Ann Courtney
b. 1967

Ryder Laurence Barnhart
b. 2011

Grey = 2nd Generation
Yellow = 3rd Generation
Blue = 4th Generation
Red = 5th Generation
Green = 6th Generation

Spouses of 4th & 5th generation are in Italics.
Dates/names are as accurate as we could find.
We apologize for any gaps.

FORWARD

Looking up-lake from Moore Point. Photo by J.R. Moore. ca. 1897

Courtney home. ca.1956

"As the chickens were busy gobbling up the pancakes and oatmeal on the porch table and granddad was running around like a wild man, your mother, June was making her entry into the world in a small log cabin up the Stehekin Valley." The year was 1918 and this was how my uncle Laurence Courtney remembered the day. At six years old, Laurence was the oldest of four children, Laurence, Curt, June and Ray, born to Hugh and Mamie Moore Courtney. That day marked the beginning of my connection to Stehekin. Currently, there are about twenty - six family members still living here, almost half of us on the original homestead of our grandparents. Our passion for these mountains and our heritage runs deep. Our great grandparents, the Moores, came to Moore Point in 1889 with that same passion. Our grandparents, the Courtneys, brought it on to Stehekin with them in 1918. Many words have been used to describe this isolated valley in Northern Washington State but the one I like best is simply home, in the truest sense of the word.

People have often asked what my connection is to the Moore – Courtney families since my last name is Barnhart. To keep it simple, my mother June was the third child born to Hugh and Mamie Moore Courtney and the only girl. June was also the only one born in the homestead cabin near the end of Company Creek Road. When she turned eighteen, June left the valley and eventually married my father, Kenny Barnhart, in 1940. They lived in Wenatchee where my sister, Mary, and I were born and went to school. Mary and I were the first two grandchildren born to Hugh and Mamie, and we got our first taste of Stehekin at a very early age: Mary in 1941 and myself in 1944.

Over the years Stehekin became our home away from home. When we weren't in Wenatchee, we were in Stehekin. My passion for these mountains and lifestyle grew as I got older; eventually I was able to move to the valley.

My first clear memory of my grandparents' farm is from the spring of 1948 when I was four years old. Mary and I were playing in the snow next to the cabin. I couldn't get over the thought that we could look down into the cabin from up on the bank. We were almost at roof level. I had never seen snow that deep. The whole idea of staying in a log cabin nearly buried in snow, deep in the woods of Stehekin, made a huge impression on me. It sounds quite insignificant now, but it was so different than where we lived in Wenatchee. When you are born into this lifestyle, the deep snow is something you grow up with. There's nothing at all unusual about it, but to a four- year-old city kid, it was mind-boggling.

My mother was born in that same log cabin. At ten years old, June took her first trip to town to visit the dentist in Chelan. The four hour boat ride down fifty-five mile Lake Chelan was filled with thoughts about what it would be like. It's interesting that her first experiences in town were just as eye-opening in a different sort of way, as ours were in Stehekin. She had never seen so many cars, buildings and different looking people in fancy clothes (fancy by her standards). She had seen these things in magazines but not firsthand. She also saw her first movie, a silent film. Awestruck by it all, she just wanted to come home. Admittedly, June was a tomboy and at that point in time, town was no place for her.

At four years old, I didn't have opinions yet on where I wanted to be. The deep snow was simply a first memory, but it was a good one. It planted the seed that grew right along with me, as I became older and started to have more experiences at the farm. I had to be in town to go to school and be at home, but clearly, my heart was in Stehekin, and luckily, a good part of our summer vacations were spent here. Winters in Wenatchee sitting in a classroom, daydreaming about Stehekin, didn't do much for my grades. Planning hiking trips, roaming the high country, building a cabin…these were the thoughts that occupied my mind more than academics.

One of my favorite places to play—and sometimes get in trouble—in Stehekin, was the leather shop. It was actually a building with a small leather shop within it, lots of things were stored there. I remember various pieces of furniture and tools all waiting to be fixed. But the leather shop was what I was attracted to. The fragrance of leather and the white pine cabinets were like a magnet to me. The drawers had all sorts of special tools and unfinished small projects. The south facing side had windows made of eisenglass, that membrane-reinforced plastic that was a forerunner to the regular visqueen that's used today. There were many projects in various stages of completion such as saddles, belts, harness straps, wallets and tool holders. The floor was covered with leftover scraps from which I always found something to put in my pocket. That scrap piece of leather was like incense. Every time I took it out of my pocket and rubbed it by my nose, it left me with the good feeling of being back in the shop. I still have a small piece, recently discovered in a long forgotten apple box labeled "Mike's childhood junk."

Other favorite places were the log barn and the shack next to it. The shack was a two-story building that my uncles, Curt and Laurence built, mostly for their bedrooms, however, it was big enough so they each had living space as well. The bottom level had a fireplace in it and the walls were papered. The building sat down in a low place right next to the barn. Instead of a ladder or stairs to the upper level there was a ramp with cleats on it; since the ramp was on higher ground, it wasn't much of an incline.

Old log barn

Mary and June Barnhart, Hugh Courtney, Muggins the dog, and Mike Barnhe at Basin Creek near Horseshoe Basin.

By the time I was old enough to remember much, the shack had seen better days. It was no longer being used as sleeping quarters. Now it was for storage and a place for the rats to call home. I remember boxes of letters that had been bundled with string that the rats had half eaten and scattered everywhere. They were several inches deep on the floor; now more like shredded paper mixed with rat droppings than the once-intended storage of personal writings of long ago. A few salvaged letters from the shack aroused my interest in our family history. What inspired a young, fairly well-to-do family from New York to settle in the remote, mountain country of the North Cascades? I can only speculate, but I'll bet it had something to do with wanting to see what's on the other side of that mountain pass; the wildness of these mountains; that driving force to explore, to see what's over the top. Those same urges that pulled me from Wenatchee to Stehekin seventy years later.

Clearing rocks for the orchard at Moore Point. ca. 1892.

Binocular & Compass

PART 1 - EARLY DAYS

The Moore - Courtney Families

Man and boy rowing at Moore Point. Steamer "Lady of the Lake" in background.

PART 1 ~ CHAPTER 1

THE MOORES

The Moore family and friends enjoying a picnic on the south facing side of Moore Point. Third from left is my grandmother Mamie Moore in her early teens. On the far right is her mother and father, Mary and J.R. Moore. ca. 1901

Michael and Maria Moore, my great-great grandparents owned and operated the Moore Hotel in Trenton Falls, New York. Originally called the Sherman Hotel, Maria's father, John Sherman gave the hotel and grounds to Michael and Maria on their wedding day. Their son, J.R. Moore and his wife Mary were the founders of the Moore Hotel on Lake Chelan in North Eastern Washington State.

Mary Moore and son Archie

J.R. Moore

Mary and J.R. Moore, my great grandparents founded the Moore Hotel in 1890 on upper Lake Chelan.

One day in 1889, my great-grandfather, J. Robert Moore, decided to leave a prospering law practice and photography business in up-state New York. His father, Michael Moore, the owner of the Moore Hotel in Trenton Falls, N.Y., had recently passed away. Robert and his young family were ready to move on to a new way of life out west. Originally, they moved to Great Falls, Montana where he planned to practice law. Not liking the severe Montana winters, he took the advice of an acquaintance and headed for the Lake Chelan area of Washington State. Mary and the children stayed in Great Falls and would follow after he found a new place for them. In the spring of 1890, he boarded the steamer at Chelan for the all day trip to Stehekin, at the head of the lake.

Moore Hotel ca. 1891

Lake Chelan is a fifty-five mile long lake located in the North Central part of the state. The small village of Stehekin lies at the upper end, about seventy miles from the Canadian border. No roads connect Stehekin to the outside world. Since white men first started coming to the region, boats have been the main mode of transportation to the roadless area. Some of the early prospectors traveled by horse, on crude, Indian trails, across rugged mountain passes. About 1891, wood-fired steamboats began running regular scheduled trips to Stehekin. The first steamboat, The Belle of Chelan, was powered by an 1866 ten horsepower Westinghouse oscillating steam engine. Using twelve cords of wood for the two day round trip, top speed for the seventy-five foot boat was about seven miles per hour.

As the steamer plied the rough waters of the narrow, winding lake, Robert was in awe of the ruggedness of the snow-covered peaks. About forty miles up the lake, a point of land came into view— the alluvial fan of a roaring creek. As the steamer approached, he

The Moore family waving farewell to guests leaving the Moore Hotel on the steamer Belle of Chelan. ca. 1900

Archie reading in the hotel.

knew this was the place he was looking for. It had the potential to become one of the regions finest destination tourist sites on the lake. At Stehekin, another hotel, the Argonaut, later called the Field Hotel, was already taking in boarders.

After getting his homestead documented and ordering lumber for the cabin, Robert sent for his wife, Mary, and two children, Archie, eleven, and Mamie, three (Mamie later became my grandmother, Mrs. Hugh Courtney). They arrived in early November only to find that Robert, still living in a tent, was also struck by the gold fever attracting others to the area. Most of the summer was wasted prospecting, delaying work on the cabin. The lumber, however, was there, so with Mary's prompting, it didn't take long to get a fairly comfortable cabin built.

Below is an excerpt from a letter addressed to Robert written by his mother, my great-great-grandmother, Maria Sherman Moore, expressing her concerns for the family's safety and well-being out west. It was written on Oct 30, 1890.

"I do hope dear Mamie (Mary was also called Mamie) and the children reached you safely, without detention or accident and that she will be pleased with the spot you have chosen for a home. There will be many trials and privations to be borne in a new place like that no doubt and I trust you will look bravely ahead and bear with them fortitude. You may rely on me to help you all in my power. I hope there are some nice people there, I am thinking of you all the time. Is there a school there? Trust Archie will put his shoulder to the wheel and make things go ahead. Trust he will like it there and see the necessity of making himself useful. Should like very much to have seen him and dear little Louise (Mamie Louise) once again. Suppose she is quite a help to mama by this time in her own way. How did they stand so long a journey, and the dear mother, she must have been terribly tired. I was thinking of her all the week. Am now doing the same and shall continue to do so until I hear that they are all safe with you.

I am most affectionately
Your grateful and loving mother
Maria Moore"

A letter written by Robert's wife to her sister, back in New York, speaks of the hardships they endured. She wrote:

"We found Robert quite well but he had not been able to put up any house when we first came here so we lived in a tent for a week. Last night was our first here in our little home which is made of rough lumber, all in one room. Just one large square room this winter will be hard for us but if we keep our health I am sure we will get along. We have a lovely spot here with the Cascade Mountains on every side. The lake is right in front of the house and we enjoy rowing and fishing. Have been feasting on venison for the past few days. When the railroad is cut through here our claim will be very valuable. We have no neighbors within ten miles of us. I trust you will write me VERY often for letters will be doubly welcome as we are so shut up from the outside world."

That small, rough-lumber cabin was the beginning of the Moore Hotel. Soon, the Moores added other rooms and a second story. Package tours from the East coast advertised all transportation included, right up to the dock at Moore Point.

Mamie Moore, my grandmother, grew up at the hotel, working right along with the men. Today, you can still see the rock walls she built, the terraced flower gardens and the old garden and hayfield that she helped clear. She loved gardening and working with the animals. At one time, she even had a pet bear, raised from a cub, when its mother was killed. The lifestyle at Moore Point suited her perfectly. Old photographs taken by her father show clearly how much she loved being there.

Winter at the Moore Hotel. ca. 1893

Mamie Moore having a laugh with one of the steers. ca. 1900

Moore family in front of sign at hotel.

Mary Moore rowing at Moore Point.

In 1903, at the young age of 16, Mamie married William Lotspiech. Two children, Harwood and Dorothy, were born from that marriage. Mamie and William moved to the Wenatchee area where he worked various jobs, and she took care of Harwood, raised a garden, and cooked for William and the orchard crews. Mamie terribly missed her family and the lifestyle at Moore Point, especially the animals. She was trying to make do, but her letters home clearly revealed the sadness she was enduring. Soon she became pregnant with Dorothy, but the marriage was failing. One day William left, never to return; Mamie never heard from him again. In 1907, after an annulment, Mamie moved back to Moore Point, continuing to work at the hotel and raising her two small children with the help of family and friends.

In 1908, another young man arrived to work for the Moores. Originally from Illinois, Hugh Courtney had been driving a freight team from Chelan Falls to Chelan when he accepted a job at the hotel. Coming west in 1904, his family lived on a little place called Sunnybank, a few miles up the lake from Chelan. In 1906, while driving a freight team up the old Knapps Hill switchbacks, Hugh's father was killed in an accident. Shortly after that, the family, all but Hugh, moved back to Illinois. About this time Robert's health started failing and he passed away on August 31, 1909. A year later, Mary became sick and died on November 3, 1910. After becoming good friends and falling in love, Hugh and Mamie were married on November tenth, of that year, one week to the day after Mary died. They moved to Chelan in 1911, after Mamie and her brother, Archie Moore, sold the hotel and property.

Moore Hotel and flower garden.

Ladder against roof of Moore Hotel.

Mamie Moores childhood sled

Moore family in tent by fire, Mamie, back row, third from left.

J.R. Moores portrait view camera

Mary and Mamie Moore – mother and daughter at work in the garden.

PART I ~ CHAPTER II

HUGH and MAMIE COURTNEY

As a long-time rock hound, Hugh had a nice collection of special rocks he'd gathered over the years from many places in the mountains around Stehekin. Showing off the rocks and explaining what they were was a favorite pastime. He had an ultraviolet light, referred to as a black light, that, when used in the dark, made the rocks look absolutely stunning. Granddad would have a group of folks over for a potluck dinner, then after dark he'd get out the black light, arrange the rocks for the best color combinations and put on a great show. It was fun to watch him and listen to the stories about his rocks.

Picnic at the Courtney Homestead. ca. 1957

Hugh Courtney, second from right with dog and apple packing crew in Chelan. ca. 1911

I woke up to the sound of granddad splitting kindling for the morning fires. Not that slow, heavy kind of splitting but the more rapid, hissing sound of the ax slicing down through dry wood, each piece snapping off, closely followed by another, and yet another. A few years later, when I started cutting my own wood, I realized that the standard by which I measured my own ability with the ax went back to those days listening to Granddad splitting kindling on the back porch. I think my first lesson came, not by watching, but from listening.

Getting the fires going was the beginning of the daily routine for granddad. During cold weather, while visiting the homestead, my sister, Mary, and I slept on the couch in the main part of the cabin so we were right in the middle of things. As we huddled under the quilts, I listened as Granddad took out his pocket knife and whittled little curled up shavings, being careful not to slice the piece off the kindling stick until there were several curled pieces all bunched up together, then he'd take it off with one, hard slice of the knife and lay it in the stove. After repeating this process two or three times, he had enough to lay larger pieces of kindling on, and the touch of a match had it going in a flash.

After the kitchen stove was started in the same fashion, I could hear the squeaky handle of the pitcher pump at the kitchen sink as he filled the hot water reservoir and a couple of tea kettles on the stove. Afterwards, the pleasant aromas of coffee, wood smoke and Prince Albert tobacco began to fill the cabin. Like a lot of men from that era, Granddad rolled his own cigarettes. I still have a can of his Prince Albert (P-A, as it was called); popping the lid off once in awhile for a good whiff is a nice way to keep some of those old memories alive.

After Hugh and Mamie were married in 1910, they worked various jobs in the lower lake Chelan area. In the days before automobiles, moving job-to-job was much different than today. Most of the jobs were on ranches, and if you were lucky, housing was available for your family. Otherwise, you moved your family as close as possible and made the trek to and from work by foot or horseback. That nomadic lifestyle was common in those days, but it still was not easy. Mamie shared with June many times over the years how tired she got of packing up and moving household goods, animals and children.

In 1915, just before Curt was born, the family moved to Chelan Falls, making several wagon trips to haul their belongings down from Chelan, four miles away. They lived near the railroad tracks and that winter one of Mamie's greatest fears was that Dorothy and Harwood, while sledding off the hill behind the house, would slide under a moving train. A few more gray hairs were added when she learned that Harwood, eleven, had once crossed the Columbia River on the ice. He made it fine, but it sure didn't help Mamie's stress level.

Laurence shared the story about Mary Lucy, an old Indian woman, who frequently walked up the tracks to beg for food. While standing at the door, waiting for Mamie to get her something, her eyes never left the cuckoo clock on the wall. She acted as if she would run if it did anything it wasn't supposed to, but it never did. Mamie always gave her food and sent her on her happy way.

Later, in the spring of 1917, after moving up to the Seegner ranch on the Antoine, a small valley about four miles north of Chelan. Hugh learned that Frank Lesh was looking for men to work in his sawmill at Stehekin. After riding up the lake, he secured the job and stayed long enough to build a small shack for the family near the mill. In May of that year he went back to Chelan, packed up Mamie and the kids once more, and moved to Stehekin. The job panned out well. Hugh took a liking to saw milling and working in the woods. He certainly wasn't afraid of hard work. The Stehekin lifestyle suited them both. At thirty-one and thirty-two years old respectively, Hugh and Mamie finally found a place to plant their roots and call home. The shack worked well for the summer, but as it turned out, they didn't have to stay there for the winter. Frank and his wife offered their home to the Courtneys while they spent the winter in California. That winter, Hugh and Mamie put their name

in for the old, abandoned William McComb homestead about a mile-and-a-half up the road from the Lesh place. It was accepted, and on April 19, 1918 with Mamie seven months pregnant with my mother June, they moved up to the homestead.

The letter below from my thirteen-year-old aunt, Dorothy, to her brother, Harwood, describes the move in detail:

"…We moved yesterday or(?) on your birthday and we had a great time. Laurence and I went down to get Mr. Inlow and caught him pretty nearly down to his place going to set bear traps way up on the mountain but he helped us anyway and we got one load up in the morning and then we had to take another load right after dinner. We took that load and the next about 5:30 in the evening. Papa had to go down after another load but Mr. & Mrs. Caldwell and John Merritt came up to drive the team back. It was about twelve o clock when we got to bed; we walked up so that made us tireder than ever. Mr. Inlow put up the stove and beds and we had to shovel the dirt out it was so deep. We couldn't bring the chickens so we had to leave them until tonight but I went and let them out and we couldn't catch all of them so Elmer Pershall and his wife get four eggs. We get four eggs every day so we have eggs for breakfast every morning and that is a great help. There are lots of mosquitoes up here. I am nearly eaten up with them.
We think our team will be up today so that we can start farming in a little while and can get things started. Mr. Washburn gave me some flower seeds and I already have some and Mr. Inlow is going to give me some pansies they are in bloom.

Well I must close,
*   Your very loving sister, Dorothy Courtney"*

McGregor Flats School. Built about 1915.

At first, they had just the one room log cabin. Dorothy and Laurence slept outdoors in a tent, Harwood was in Chelan going to school, and Hugh, Mamie and Curt all slept on a folding bunk bed built in one corner of the cabin. Later that summer and fall, with the help of Fred and Dewey Merritt, a kitchen, back porch and woodshed were added. A Sibley stove sat in a frame on the dirt floor of the cabin for heat. Sibley's are a large, Civil War-era cone-shaped stove with no bottom and a six-inch opening at the top for a stovepipe. An army officer, Lt. Sibley, originally designed it to be used in the Sibley tent, a twenty-person tent he also designed. The stoves were cheap to build and easy to transport since they had no bottoms and were stackable. In Stehekin, the Sibley stove found many uses around the farms. They were ideal for burning stumps when clearing land. Many a night the family huddled around the stove as the wind whistled outside. Apparently, Fred's dog, Shorty, liked the stove, too. Whenever he came in the cabin, the first thing he did was pee on the stove! What a smell and something Mamie put a stop to in short order!

The first year at the homestead, Dorothy and Harwood went to school at the McGregor Flats School otherwise known as the Cronk cabin, located right across the river from the Courtney homestead. Rather than going down to the bridge and back up the other side, Hugh dropped a large tree across the river allowing the kids a much easier walk to school. The following year, school was moved to an old cabin owned by Fred Bowen near the bridge crossing over to the Lesh Sawmill, on what later became the Wilson property. Later, Barney Zell donated land near Rainbow Creek where, in 1921, a new school was built. Since children lived at both ends of the valley, it made a lot of sense to have a school more centrally located, especially since most often the kids had to walk to school. In the winter, when the snow got deep, Hugh went

Hugh Courtney's mother

ahead of the kids with his snowshoes to break trail; but as we all know, walking in boots on a snowshoe trail doesn't always work so well. Breaking through the snow down to your knees every few steps (we call it post-holing) turns into a lot of work. At six years old, it was quite a struggle for Laurence.

In the fall of 1919, Mamie was expecting another child. Wanting to be closer to a doctor this time, the family moved to Winesap, a small community of ranches about halfway between Chelan and Entiat, where Hugh found work. On the tenth of May 1920, Ray, the newest and last member of the family, was born. In June, as soon as school got out, the family moved back to Stehekin. This time, however, to be closer to school and the boat landing, they spent a few winters down at the Merritt place, about two-and-a-half miles from Stehekin

Shortly after moving back to Stehekin in 1920, Hugh took a job with the Forest Service, scouting out and surveying several of the trails leading out of the valley, including the trails down Bridge Creek and the Agnes Valley. He continued to work for the Forest Service for several summers, spending the winters trapping, usually up Company Creek, a good drainage for quality fur, and the trailhead was only two miles from home. He built a trapping cabin about six miles up the drainage, just below Hilgard Creek. As Curt and Laurence and later, Ray, got old enough, they also helped with the trapping. When asked what animals they trapped, Laurence replied, "anything that was stupid enough to get caught." Marten, Ermine and an occasional Mink were most often caught. A typical trip up to the cabin would last three or four days—two days travel in and out and two days at the cabin. Their trap lines ran above and below the cabin, roughly following the creek about a mile each way. After clearing and resetting the traps, they'd spend the next day back at the cabin skinning and stretching the furs.

Mamie Courtney with Mary Barnhart. 1942

Courtney homestead cabin showing Hugh and Mamie's bedroom, 1938

*Flower bin and bread board given to Mamie in 1903
as a wedding gift from her father J.R. Moore.*

Living in the valley with very limited income, folks made a lot of their own tools and equipment. Early on, Hugh started making snowshoes. Soon, most everyone in the family had a pair. The best wood seemed to be Tamarack. Hugh steamed the two pieces for the frame, attaching them at the tail with a small bolt sawed off and peened over to make a rivet. One pitch-black night, Hugh, Laurence and Curt were snowshoeing home from Dorothy and Charley's place down the road. Carrying a kerosene lantern, Hugh was leading, with Curt following and Laurence bringing up the rear. All of a sudden Hugh let out a yell, falling face first into the snow. As he fell, the lantern flew from his hand, sailing out through the woods, burying itself deep in the fifteen inches of new snow that had fallen the night before. Curt had been following too close behind Granddad, hooking the toe of his snowshoe over the bolt sticking out of the tail of Hugh's snowshoe—a new pair that didn't have the bolt cut off yet—taking him down in a heartbeat. Hugh often got pretty worked up in times like this, so it made quite a scene as the three of them were flailing around in the deep snow looking for the lost lantern while Hugh was cussing up a storm.

It wasn't long before the family bought two milk cows to go with the chickens and team of horses. Hugh rented the horses to the Forest Service while working on trails, as well as using them for making improvements on the homestead. Mamie took care of the cows and chickens. She loved working with animals, having lots of experience from living at Moore Point. A letter from Curt during the war when Hugh and Mamie were alone at the farm read in part…

"I know that chores must take up most of your days. You always did take better care of all the animals than anybody up there."

Kenny Barnhart and Laurence Courtney stacking timbers cut in Courtney mill. 1943

Mamie and Hugh Courtney at the homestead, 1942

And, when it came to milking, Mamie wouldn't let anyone else do it. She claimed the others didn't get all the milk out. One interesting thing she did was name the hens after people she knew. That was all fine and dandy as long as she didn't call them by name when one of their namesakes happened to be around. Their Plymouth Red Rock rooster had a terrible dislike for women. He chased June and Mamie whenever he caught them out in the open, pecking and scratching their legs. One time he stood outside the outhouse and wouldn't let Mamie out. Chasing them once too often, Mamie had enough. The next day he found himself on the stove in a pot of noodles.

The cows had their own personalities. When the river was low, they often crossed over to the other side, making it hard to find them. One cow named Betty was more or less the leader, so they decided to put a bell on her; that way, once they found her, the others were usually near by. But Betty had a trick up her sleeve. About the time she figured they were looking for her, she hid in a brushy thicket, standing perfectly still so the bell wouldn't make a sound. Even though they laughed about it later, it wasn't a laughing matter at the time. Many hours were spent hunting cows. At least once, Betty stayed out all night. Mamie was worried sick that something would get her.

In 1927, Laurence purchased the first family car, a 1917 Chevrolet 4-90 touring car. He traded a months work with O.P. Maxwell in exchange for the car. O.P., a bachelor, had a large farm and hayfields up at nine mile, where the Stehekin Valley Ranch is today. Laurence and Curt were the most mechanically minded of the family, so learning to drive the car was natural for them. It was a different story for Granddad.

June remembered one of the driving lesson days:

"Dad was so funny! He just couldn't get the hang of it. We were all jerking back and forth laughing at him, but he took it all in good humor. He was just one of us kids some of the time."

Needless to say, most of the driving was left to the boys.

Granddad's great sense of humor almost cost losing the cabin to a fire in the summer of 1956. When I was twelve, a friend and I came up to camp for a few weeks to tear down what was left of a small garage my dad built several years before. The record-setting snows of the previous winter had knocked the garage down, and we figured this was a good opportunity to come up and hang out with our sisters and a couple other girls who worked for Beryl at the restaurant. But Granddad insisted that we use his cabin. He was now living in the new house that was built for him and Grandma, and the cabin was not being used.

After Mamie died, Hugh had continued to live in the old cabin for several years. Granddad wasn't ready to leave his familiar routine, away from where he and Mamie spent so many years together, even though it was only a few feet away from the new house.

We decided to take Granddad up on his offer to use the cabin. The thought of staying in a tent for that long lost out to the luxuries of a cabin. When we arrived at the homestead, he took us in the cabin to show us the ropes and cautioned us about the dampers on the kitchen stove. Since the roof was cedar shakes, fire from stovepipe sparks was always a threat. Granddad sternly warned us about the dangers of leaving the draft and damper open on the cook stove, as it would get too hot and send sparks out onto the dry, shake roof.

The cat by the kitchen window at the homestead 1935

Two cows and Sally the horse near the shack, 1935.

Cream Seperator

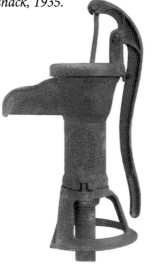

Pitcher Pump

One day, we went over to the other house to take showers and visit with Granddad. As I was walking out the door after my shower, I saw smoke coming from the roof of the cabin. Sure enough, we had forgotten the cardinal rule of closing the damper, and the roof was on fire. Granddad was not one to take emergencies lightly, and this was no exception. He let out a yell and off we went, grabbing buckets on the way. There wasn't a real water system for the new house, just an elevated water tank that was filled as needed, with a gas-driven pump. It was fine for showers and domestic use but nowhere near enough volume and pressure for putting out a fire.

On the way over, I realized that the pants I put on after my shower were huge. I must have grabbed the wrong ones. They wouldn't stay up at all without holding on to them, but there wasn't time to change, as the roof was crackling away. Hugh had a permanent ladder on the roof for such occasions. This wasn't the first time.

We started filling buckets at the pitcher pump and carrying them up the ladder. As I started up with a bucket of water, I needed both hands; as soon as I took my hand off my pants, they started to fall down. Granddad started laughing uncontrollably! He seemed to be more entertained by that than concerned with the fire. It must have been a sight, three of us pumping water like crazy, Granddad in a near panic and laughing his head off at the same time, and my pants falling down. Of course his antics would make me laugh too, so I really don't know how we managed to put that fire out, but we did. I don't remember much about what my friend was doing. Most likely he was doing the bulk of the work. A few days later, after things had settled down, I had my first lesson in splitting shakes. Granddad had a few shake bolts nearby and we got busy making new shakes and repairing the roof.

In the late 1930s, after a failed partnership with his son-in-law, Charley Byrd, in the sawmill business, Hugh and the boys set up their own sawmill at the homestead. The homestead papers state that an estimated million board feet of timber was on the 53-acre site, considerably more than even some of the larger, 160-acre allotments. Operating on a shoestring budget and just getting started was not an easy task. Setting up the mill was one thing; getting the logs to the mill was quite another. Various methods were used including home-made drum winches powered by old Model T truck engines chained to a tree, a team of horses for the smaller logs, and renting a tractor for the larger ones. All of the trees were felled and bucked up using crosscut saws and axes. A wooden flume was built to bring water out of Battalion Creek as a means to float the sawdust out into a settling pond, away from the saw. When the mill wasn't running, the water was diverted to one of Grandmother's two large gardens.

Among other things, Hugh was one of the best barbers in the valley, so it wasn't uncommon for someone to show up needing a haircut. One day, when the mill was running and several crew were all working, Pete Miller came up wanting a haircut. True to Granddad's style, he said *"Sure, no problem. We'll shut the mill down for a break and I'll cut your hair."* This didn't set well with the hired crew that was working, since they were being paid by the amount of lumber they cut, not by the hour. To kill time, they busied themselves by cleaning up around the mill and checking the machinery. One of the men checked the oil and saw that it was low, so Laurence went for a gallon of oil and filled it back up. Only then did he realize that he'd just poured the radiator full of oil. Turns out that both fill spouts for the oil and water were fairly close together, but only the oil filler had a cap on it. The radiator didn't have one. Whoever checked the oil took the cap off and set

Toboggan Used for Hauling Feed to Hungry Livestock

H. L. Courtney, who lives seven miles beyond the head of Lake Chelan, has a problem in securing feed for his three cows and two calves. Courtney recently ordered two tons of baled hay which came up to the head of the lake by boat, from there he was able to haul the hay 3½ miles up the road to the Harry Buckner ranch. But from there on, he had to use a different method to get the hay the other 3½ miles to his place.

His problem was solved when he, with snowshoes, pulled a bale at a time on a toboggan. He had to make that 3½ mile trip 31 times before the hay was all at his ranch. The county superintendent's office has received word from that region that during the first week in February, 41 inches of snow fell.

it on the radiator pipe just for convenience, so when Laurence got there with the oil he, without thinking, took the cap off and poured the oil in, only to realize after the fact that he'd just poured it in the radiator. About this time, Hugh came back from the haircut and heard the commotion. His arrival on the scene didn't help matters. As anyone who knew this bunch could imagine, the air turned blue and stayed that way for the rest of the day. And of course, the crew went home and no more lumber was cut until they got the radiator cleaned out.

When the logging got into full swing, Mamie put her foot down about the twenty or so large Douglas fir trees around the cabin. She wanted the trees to stay, but opposition was strong. They were worth a lot more as lumber than the stately giants that Mamie so loved. I still can't believe she won, but according to my mother, there were several heated discussions about those trees. To this day, the trees are still standing, thanks to the stubbornness of my grandmother.

The war years were hard on Hugh and Mamie. Curt was drafted in late 1941 and Ray in June of 1942. Laurence and Harwood were working at the Holden Mine, leaving my grandparents alone at the farm—my mother had left in 1936. Granddad was trying to keep the mill going with hired help and occasionally Laurence, when he could get away from the mine. Grandmother had all the animals to take care of plus her gardens, cooking, washing, cleaning, milking, separating, and churning butter and cheese. It never ended. She loved to work, but she also never knew when to quit. The uncertainty of the war and the well-being of her boys also was cause for worry. Having two sons in the army not only left them shorthanded but put them under a lot of stress as well. She worried constantly and wrote letters most every day to both of

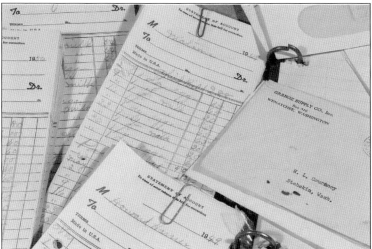

them. And they wrote back just as often. Their letters home were full of encouragement and love, but trying to remind their parents not to work too hard fell on deaf ears.

Mamie was having back problems also. The hard work and stress were beginning to show on her. On top of that, Hugh started having indigestion trouble that limited his activities. Clearly, they needed help on a regular basis. Laurence had to keep his job at the mine since it was a defense job and kept him from being drafted. That way, he could get small blocks of time to come home and help. My father also had a defense job in Wenatchee. He worked a deal with the local draft board and his boss to spend the better part of the summers of 1942 and '43 at Stehekin, helping with the mill. Since it was officially considered a hardship for Hugh and Mamie to have two of their sons in the military, the board was sympathetic to his request. My mother helped Mamie with the gardens and the rest of the chores. Curt and Ray also managed to get short leaves from the army the summer of 1942. For a while, anyway, there was a lot of help at the farm. In 1944 Curt was granted a hardship medical discharge from the army for his lingering back problems and to help out at home. It was a great relief to Hugh and Mamie.

After the war was over in 1945, Ray was finally on his way home. Having the boys home again meant the world to Mamie and Hugh. Much talk about plans for a new house for Mamie was finally put into motion. It was built just upvalley a few feet from the old house. Laurence built a thirty-foot water tower for a constant, pressurized flow of water to the house. Life would certainly be easier for Grandma with hot and cold running water, but getting the house finished was something that didn't happen right away. The boys all got busy with their own lives and endeavors, and the short blocks of time getting together to work on the house were

Hugh Courtney in the outhouse trail, 1956

getting fewer and farther between. Running the mill, trapping, and helping out with the daily chores took up most of the free time. Mamie's dairy business also was growing. Her well-kept account books listed twenty-seven regular customers for the period 1945 to 1950 buying eggs, milk, cheese, butter, cream, and cottage cheese.

Mamie's health continued to deteriorate and trips down to the doctor were becoming more frequent. On November 3, 1950, at sixty-four years old, she passed away in the Chelan Hospital. I was six that year and don't have a lot of memories of the funeral. Later, from stories, letters, articles and journals and photographs, I got to know my grandmother. Walking over the same ground here on the homestead; seeing McGregor Mountain as she saw it, and laughing to myself about her once telling my mother how she wondered if the fire lookout up there could see her peeing behind the woodshed; I realized how dedicated she was to her family; how hard she worked and her love for animals and gardening…and whistling. Mamie loved to whistle while she worked and was good at it. Only one of her children, Ray, carried on that tradition, once comparing their style of whistling to braiding leather, over one and under one. It is sad that she never got to live in the new house, but who knows? The transition may have been hard for her.

Over the next fourteen years, Hugh continued to live at the farm, selling the animals and settling in to a life of retirement, particularly enjoying his life-long hobby of geology or "rock hounding" as he liked to call it. The new house finally got finished, and he moved over a little at a time. I remember having lunch with him once in a while. He was a great cook, and I always looked forward to being there. Granddad had a pretty regular routine at lunchtime. On his old tube type radio, he tuned in Paul Harvey news. For the next fifteen minutes during lunch we listened, that is, until the first controversial thing like religion or politics came up. Then, he was off and running. You might as well shut the radio off because he had more than enough to say to fill up that fifteen minutes. And, he was loud, a common trait of old timers with hearing problems. He'd let out a string of profanities and rant and rave. It was all I could do to keep a straight face. I knew the drill pretty well. After a few minutes, he'd settle back down and we'd laugh about it and carry on.

Hugh made regular trips to Wenatchee during the winters, staying with us for a week or so to take care of errands and business. It was always a treat to see him and listen to his stories…and to watch him as he watched the Red Skelton Show on television. The show was a comedy hour with a lot of crazy skits that kept us laughing, but watching Granddad and how he reacted to the show was much better than the show itself. I'll never forget the way he sat on the edge of his chair, rolling a cigarette and watching the program. When a particularly funny skit was taking place he'd start laughing, then coughing almost uncontrollably, then without fail he'd dump the tobacco out of his half rolled smoke and down it went, on Mom's nice carpet. He'd start cussing, then laughing and I'd have to leave the room because it was about the funniest thing I had ever seen. My parents didn't think so, but it sure got me going.

As time went on, Hugh's trips to town were to see the doctor. The persistent cough had worsened to the point where lung cancer was suspected. Our fears were realized when x-rays and testing proved that to be true. It was a sad day, and as hard as I tried to understand, I couldn't get a grip on it. Hugh had such a presence here in the valley. After all, he and Mamie were some of the original people here. Their way of life suited me to a T. I always wanted to forget town and move in with Granddad. In a way, he was more

Hugh and Mamie in the garden. ca. 1943

of a father to me than my own. He could teach me the things that meant so much more than what town had to offer.

The winter of 1963-'64, Hugh started chemotherapy at Wenatchee Valley Clinic, followed by radiation. The treatments weren't helping, though, and his condition worsened. In early 1964 he moved to a nursing home since Mom could no longer take care of him at our house. Curt was building the new Boatel at the landing, where I was working part-time, dividing my time between Stehekin and Wenatchee. On one especially memorable and sad visit with Hugh, he asked, *"Is there no hope for me? Won't I ever get to go home again?"* Those words cut through me like a hot knife through butter. How do you answer that question? At nineteen, I stood there, not knowing what to say. About that time, a nurse came in, so I didn't have to struggle for the words. But I couldn't stop the tears. Here was one of the men I admired most, dying, and I couldn't do a thing about it.

Around March 1, 1964 I visited my grandfather for what turned out to be the last time. I had come to town to get my back looked at from a fall. My mother had been bringing Hugh home- cooked oatmeal for breakfast since he didn't like what they served at the nursing home. She and I went together that morning, spending an hour or so with him while he ate. That time, I remember his lack of concern for his own welfare but being quite interested in how my back was. He talked about how our family had been plagued with bad backs for generations, mentioning his own struggles with it. The visit was pleasant, but we somehow knew the end was near.

"Take care of yourself, Mike," he said.
I was choked up, but managed to reply, *"Thanks, and you too."*

Nine days later, on March 10, 1964, Granddad passed away.

Hugh Courtrney at Laurence and Lona's wedding, 1955

PART II ~ SIBLINGS

Laurence	1912 ~ 1986
Curtice	1915 ~ 2000
Katherine June	1918 ~ 2002
James Ray	1920 ~ 1982
Harwood Lotspiech*	1904 ~ 1968
Dorothy Lotspiech*	1905 ~ 1984

Harwood and Dorothy are children from Mamie's first marriage to William Lotspiech. Hugh unofficially adopted the two children and raised them as his own.

Stehekin Landing about 1945

Laurence and Muggins at the Courtney Homestead house. ca. 1948

Part II ~ Chapter I

Laurence Courtney
1912 ~ 1986

My first memory of Laurence was out in the front yard of the old cabin. I must have been four or five years old. The details are sketchy, but as I recall, one of the cows was tied to a tether in the grass. Laurence cut two holes in the top of an old fedora hat and placed it over the short horns sticking out of its head. I remember the cow not liking it, but Laurence was getting a big kick out of it. He loved animals but he also liked to tease them, *"Just a little"* he used to say, *"to get 'em going."*

This is his story:

"It was the early spring of 1920. We had moved to Winesap, a small collection of farms about half way between Chelan and Entiat, as Mom was pregnant with Ray and wanted to be closer to a doctor. My brother and I were sledding up on a hill behind the house. That's when I tried to cut my head off on a barbwire fence. There was about two feet of snow but the shady spots had a thick crust and were real slippery. We were being daredevils and climbed way up on this steep hill. Just as we started down, Dad came out on the back porch and yelled at us to stop. We couldn't see any reason to stop. Well, here was this barbwire fence at the bottom sticking out of the snow about eight inches, that's why. We were lying down on the sled, me on the bottom and Curt on top. I hit that doggone fence with my neck and just slid along. It piled us up and Dad came running up the hill. I knew I was hurt but didn't know how bad. And luckily, it wasn't very bad, although the main arteries were exposed and you could see them. I'll never forget how scared Dad was. He thought I'd had it. But after he saw that I wasn't going to die, he hiked clear down to Entiat to get a doctor. When they got back it took fourteen stitches to patch me up, but I'm none the worse for wear."

Laurence told me this story on one of my many visits in the early 1960s. As with all the family, he was a great storyteller and always had plenty to say about experiences growing up, mostly in Stehekin. Laurence was the first child born to Hugh and Mamie Courtney. In 1917, at age five, he moved to Stehekin with his family where his father had taken a job working in the Lesh sawmill about five miles up the valley on the Company Creek side of the river. It wasn't long before Laurence was able to help out with the chores and eventually work for other folks in the valley. One of his first jobs outside the family was working for O.P. Maxwell at his ranch at nine-mile. Maxwell, a bachelor, had nine dairy cows,

Laurence, Ray, Curt and June (hiding) standing by homestead cabin. ca. 1921

Curt and Laurence dusting erasers at the Rainbow Falls School. ca. 1923

a large garden and farmed about forty acres in hay. He was always looking for help and gave some of the young people around the valley their first paying jobs. While growing up, Laurence worked for Mac (as he was called) on several occasions, but his first job almost became his last. As the story goes, Mac asked ten-year-old Laurence to hoe out his strawberries, a large, beautiful patch that was his pride and joy. Well, Laurence took it literally and went to work hoeing out the strawberries, only to find out later when Mac came to check on him that he meant to hoe out the weeds in between the rows, not the plants themselves. Laurence later said he never could understand why he wanted him to take out all those nice strawberry plants. Mac chewed him out good sending him back home. He figured this was the end of his short career with O.P. Maxwell, but it wasn't long before the old man cooled off and decided to give Laurence another try. Next time, he would say exactly what he meant when giving instructions to young Laurence.

School buildings, teachers and students moved a lot in those days, and Laurence was no exception. Until the new school was built near Rainbow Falls in 1921, classes were held in several locations, depending where the most children were and the availability of a building. At least part of a year school was held at Moore Point to accommodate the children there and the Carter girls from Four Mile Creek. Laurence's early schooling is hard to track. He may have started the first grade in Stehekin but finished it in Winesap while the family was living there waiting for Ray to be born. For sure, he started the second grade back in Stehekin in March 1921, just as the teacher, Miss Leota Patterson, was beginning her second term of teaching in Stehekin. The "new" school of 1921, near Rainbow Falls, still stands today. It houses the school museum and is on the National Register of Historic Places.

Below is an excerpt from Miss Patterson's journal on seeing the valley and school for the first time in April of 1920.

"News of the coming of the teacher preceded me and when the boat docked most of the inhabitants were there to meet me. There were no cars at Stehekin, only a spring buggy and team. Barney Zell, the owner and Mr. Stanley, who I learned was the father of the three pupils who would comprise the school, escorted me to Rainbow Lodge, where I would live for the school term.

Mr. Stanley drove me on up the valley to view the school and meet his family. On the way, the subject of rattlesnakes came up. 'We do have rattlesnakes,' he remarked.'But don't be alarmed by them. Get a club and finish them off… always finish them off. It is an unwritten law in any rattler country,' he stressed."

"The school was a small, log building, at the foot of a mountain so tall I found it necessary to throw my head way back to see its top. It was on a small flat beneath great pine trees. Amid such tremendous surroundings, everything on such a gigantic scale, it looked small indeed. The one room of the school was meagerly furnished with a few seats and desks, a homemade teacher's desk, and shelves with very few books. The windows looked out on the magnificent mountain and the great sighing pines filling the air with their scent. Through the trees, one could catch glimpses of the Stehekin River."

On her second year of teaching, Leota had nine students: Curt Courtney, Webert Stanley and Fern Hart first grade; Laurence Courtney and Allen Stanley second grade; Vernice Stanley and Jim Weaver third grade, and Dorothy Courtney and Donald Rice in the eighth grade. Donald's attendance during his school years was very sporadic, resulting in repeating several grades. His age listed for the spring term of 1921 was nineteen. Donald's biggest obstacles were his sudden outbursts of made-up words and laughing uncontrollably over seemingly nothing. One time during one of his laughing spells, the teacher asked what was so funny and he told her he had a headache. Another time Donald starting talking to himself loudly about clubbing "humpies", a name given to the spawning freshwater salmon that migrated up the Stehekin River every fall. Occasionally, after one of his tirades, he would suddenly jump from his desk and run out the door, not to be seen for the rest of the day…or several days for that matter. His antics kept the rest of the class in such an uproar that the teacher was usually in no hurry to have him back. Most people weren't afraid of Donald…his outbursts were never in anger, but as Laurence put it, *"He was just different. When Donald started laughing and carrying on, everyone laughed and it was hard to conduct classes with him around."*

Right after World War I, times were hard for the Courtney family. There wasn't much work, and food was scarce. My grandparents were boarding Oscar Hart's dog while Oscar was gone for the winter; with their dog, Beans, and six people, they went through forty-nine sacks of potatoes and three deer. They had no flour, but instead shared mill feed with the cow. They sifted it until it was fine enough for Mamie to make bread. Hugh and Bob Pershall split a one hundred pound bag of sugar that cost twenty-seven dollars, as neither could afford the full price. Laurence remembered their school lunches during those lean times:

"Our school lunches consisted mostly of fried egg sandwiches. Occasionally, we would have applesauce or an apple and later on when we got thermos bottles we had hot chocolate. I used to trade my fried egg sandwiches to Jim Weaver for his jam sandwiches as we

did not have jam and Jim's mother evidently wouldn't give him fried eggs".

Laurence was ten when he had his second serious accident, chopping a section out of his hand.

"I had my hand lying on a chunk of wood, chopping with the ax, and it just hit the side of my thumb. I packed a sore hand around for a good long while, then, it got infected. But then, when I was nineteen, I finished the job. I got the whole thumb there finally. It was the same kind of a deal, splitting wood and not moving my hand out of the way fast enough. I like to bled to death that time because there are two little arteries that come down your wrist and nobody knew how to stop the darned thing from bleeding. This was on the 30th of April and we were getting ready to go to work for the Forest Service on May first. We were chopping up a bunch of extra wood for Mom when Curt came along and asked me to quit and go fishing with him. I said I wanted to finish this one piece and that's the one that got me. Anyway, they got me down to the head of the lake and there was a guy there with a pretty fast boat…if it was ready to go. So, he dug the motor out and got it all ready to go and cranked it up but it wouldn't run right. We got down to Lucerne and there was a guy from the mine with a fast boat so he took me on to 25-Mile-Creek. Then, we had to drive all the way around to Manson, since that was where the doctor was. I came out from under the ether at 2:00 in the afternoon. Six hours from the time I whacked it off."

In 1927, when Laurence was in the eighth grade, he took time out from school to work for the Forest Service on trail maintenance at Prince Creek. They paid three dollars a day and board which was pretty good for a fifteen-year-old back then. The work involved relocating some of the Lakeshore Trail. That same year he bought

Curt, Hugh, Mamie, Laurence and June in the family car. ca. 1932

his first car (and the first family car.) It was a 1917 4-90 Chevrolet touring car for the price of fifty dollars; exactly what O.P. Maxwell owed him for a months work that involved working in the hayfield and milking the cows. Having never driven a car, he asked Mac to help him learn a little bit about it. Those were the days of hand cranks for getting the engine started. Laurence crawled into the driver's seat, set the spark and throttle controls, and Mac went out in front to turn the crank. The car started up with the first spin, but unbeknownst to him, Laurence had the car in gear and the clutch out, so as soon as the engine started, it lurched forward, darned near running over Mac. While it missed him, it didn't miss a log lying in front, and the car jumped right up over it, high-centering itself. It doesn't take much imagination to know how that little episode ended. After things cooled off, they got out the jack and pulled the log out, and no, it wasn't the end for Laurence and Mac. He managed to get off the hook again.

When school got out in June, Laurence went to work for Chelan County on Stehekin road maintenance. Later that summer, he decided to try the fire lookout job for the Forest Service on Boulder Butte. Laurence described his living situation:

"My housing was a tent, anchored with guy wires so the wind wouldn't blow it away. The pay was $110 a month but I had to furnish my own groceries. About every three weeks Curt would bring my supplies in on a pack horse, a nine mile trip from the valley floor. For water, I had to walk down the hill into the basin to a little lake. The distance was about a mile straight down and straight up so I certainly conserved water."

In 1928, Laurence, his dad, and just about anyone else that wanted to work, got jobs logging and clearing the head of the lake. The

Camp 5 at Stehekin Flats 1926. Notice stacks of Sibley stoves for the tents. Photo courtesy Chelan County PUD

Camp 5 at Stehekin Flats 1926. Photo courtesy Chelan County PUD

lake was being raised twenty-one feet by the new hydroelectric dam being built in Chelan. The area logged was about a mile long, from Purple Point up to where the Buehler cabin sits today. Since there weren't any sawmills nearby, and transporting the logs was not cost effective, the huge piles of logs, some as high as fifty feet, were burned on the spot. The contractor, Grant Smith and Company, employed up to 260 men on the yearlong project. Large tent camps, resembling an army camp, were spread over the area being cleared.

In the fall of 1929, Laurence took a job with Frank Hubbard, tearing down the Moore Hotel, the one his grandfather had built in 1889, and moving to higher ground. They were getting their feet wet from the rising lake as the last of the lumber was moved further back up the hill. Laurence worked well into the winter helping rebuild the hotel. The following spring, he worked again for Mr. Hubbard, taking care of his stock.

Laurence was a very hard worker and strong as an ox, but when he wasn't working, his favorite pastime was sitting by the radio, smoking and listening to "The Shadow" and other old programs. Mom recalled times when Granddad would need help with something, but if Laurence was listening to a program you couldn't budge him from the chair. In those days before TV, radio programs were very popular and Laurence was a true follower of the trend. I think he owned that corner where the home-made chair and side desk table was located. The antenna wire stretched about 200 feet from the top of a large fir tree upvalley, to one of the big trees in the front yard. From there, through a series of white porcelain insulators nailed to the ends of rafters, the wire came in through a hole in the log wall and hooked to the radio, an old battery type Westinghouse. I remember, as a kid, sitting in the chair and

The last of Camp 5 1926. The two frame structures are from acquired lands of previous homesteaders. Photo Courtesy Chelan County PUD

The rebuilt Moore Hotel after it was moved to higher ground in 1927. The original hotel fireplace is shown at left. ca. 1954

admiring all the stuff on the little desktop. Ashtrays, hand scribbled notes listing the times of favorite programs, books, pens, knives, a couple of Alka Seltzer bottles filled with little screws, and always, a can of PA and a package or two of cigarette papers. Really, this was my favorite place in the cabin also. The corner was a special place where you could let your imagination go while listening, under the dim light of a kerosene lamp, to stories like "The Lone Ranger" or "Gunsmoke." I understood why Laurence didn't want to be bothered. But, to be fair, all three of the boys worked on "the corner." I never knew what events led up to who actually got to sit there on any given night, but Laurence was the oldest, the biggest and the toughest, so that probably settled any disputes.

Trapping was another source of income for the family. Nearly every winter they trapped marten, weasel and mink during the thirty-day season. After skinning, stretching and drying the furs, they were sold, often to Sears Roebuck, since they paid the best price. A marten could bring as much as thirty-five dollars, but prices varied from year-to-year and sometimes would go as low as fifteen.

Laurence had another accident coming down Company Creek one winter. This one almost took his life. Rain had fallen on top of dry snow and made footing pretty slippery. Hugh cut steps with his hatchet on the steep terrain going up, but coming back down, it was hard to use the steps. On that particular trip, Laurence slipped and shot like a bullet downhill toward a forty-foot cliff. He saw a rock sticking out and was able to guide himself into it just three feet from going over the cliff.

In 1933, Laurence joined the CCC (Civilian Conservation Corps), a program started by the Roosevelt Administration to put people back to work after the Great Depression. His job was working on the Manson Reclamation Road from Coyote Creek up to Navarre Basin to connect with the Cooper Mountain Road.

After working various jobs over the next four years, Laurence went to work for Howe Sound Mining Company up at Holden. His first job there was cutting piling for the new dock at Lucerne, then as a truck driver hauling freight from Lucerne to Holden. In April 1938, Laurence hauled the fist load of ore from the mine to the barge at Lucerne. He stayed on at the mine through the war years. Because of not having a thumb, he didn't have to go in the military but did have to work at a defense job, which the mine was. In 1945 he left Holden and went to work for Inland Petroleum driving

Laurence sitting in his ore truck at Lucerne. 1942

tanker truck back and forth from Seattle to Wenatchee.

That job only lasted a year, and in 1946 he came back to Stehekin to help Hugh and Curt in the sawmill and work on the "new house," a project all the family was trying to finish as a gift for Mamie.

Laurence returned to work for Chelan County on the Stehekin Road in 1949, then ended up going to work for Horse Shoe Basin Mining and Development Company as a cat operator, hauling freight and running the tramway—two long cable systems used to haul freight from the lower basin to the upper basin at the 6000 foot level. The first cable was 900 feet long and took material up to the edge of the upper basin. The second line was 6000 feet long and took about an hour and twenty minutes to haul a load up to the mine. The season was pretty short due to the heavy snows in that area. By the time they could get up there in the summer and get squared away, they only had about three months to work in order to get back out before the heavy snows came. Laurence worked a couple of seasons before the company finally went broke. He always had plenty to say about how things were mismanaged.

This is what he said about the way money was being spent up at the mine:

"As usual, they would hire somebody with all kinds of knowledge but very little common sense. Dad called them educated fools. They'd go up there with $150,000 and hardly make a showing with what they'd done. The darn fools always had a better way of doing things but their ideas hardly ever worked."

Military surplus mine truck at Rouses Camp. Now called Basin Creek camp. ca.1949

Laurence on Cat working on the road near High Banks at six mile. ca. 1950

Upper Horseshoe Basin tram winch. ca. 1949

Laurence's lifestyle took a major change in 1954 when Lona Miller came to Stehekin as a reporter for the Wenatchee Daily World. Somehow, he got the job of escorting her around the valley for her story and photographs. Perhaps Curt's wife, Beryl, had a hand in that. She knew Lona, but she also knew that Laurence needed a good woman in his life. As the story goes, after Lona got back to Wenatchee and developed the film, she sent Laurence copies of the photos and her flattering article about him and Stehekin. Not knowing what to do next, he asked Beryl, *"What should I do?"* Without hesitation, Beryl, a very direct and to-the-point person, came right back with, *"Well, I'd get right down there and take her out to dinner".*

Indeed, it was a big change for Laurence. Nobody could believe that he was really settling down and getting married. In 1955 they said their vows in a Wenatchee Church, formally ending his work in the Stehekin Valley. I was eleven at the time, and I remember telling Lona she was my favorite aunt. I had several favorite aunts, but Lona was an exceptionally nice person and for what little my young mind could comprehend about such matters, I figured there must be something special about them both to have found each other. She was thirty-eight, he was forty-two, and they went on to have two fine sons, Joe and Marvin, and several grandchildren.

Laurence and Lona settled in Wenatchee where Lona continued working for the *Wenatchee Daily World*. Laurence retired in 1977 from W I Forest Products in Cashmere as a master mechanic. In 1984, I took Laurence and my mother, June, down to Moore Point to reminisce about our family ties there. Laurence had many good memories of working for Mr. Hubbard, the man who bought the Moore property from Mamie and Archie.

Laurence and Lona's wedding photo. 1955

We took several photos and walked over the grounds, listening to stories about his time there. It was the last visit to the old home site for Laurence.

Even when he was dying from cancer, Laurence kept his extraordinary sense of humor. While at a Seattle hospital for tests, the front of his hospital gown came open and he quickly covered himself up. The nurse doing the tests said: *"Oh don't worry about that, I've seen them all."* Always quick to respond, Laurence replied, *"Well, you haven't seen mine."*

Laurence died in 1986 at the age of seventy-four.

June Courtney Barnhart and Laurence Courtney.
Brother and sister reminising at the old Moore Hotel site, 1984

June Courtney Barnhart, Hugh Courtney, Lona Miller Courtney,
Laurence, Joe and Marvin Courtney. ca. 1961

Part II - Chapter II

Curtice Courtney
1915 - 2000

Sitting at the old U shaped lunch counter at Curt and Beryl's coffee shop waiting for the boat with Curt and some of the old-timers was a favorite mid-day event: Dad Imus fidgeting with his cigarette holder; Paul Bergman having his customary piece of Washington nut pie à la mode; Beryl flipping hamburgers on the gas grill in the corner, laughing and adding her two cents worth to a joke someone just told; Gladys Simmerman scolding her husband, Bob, after one of his long-winded exaggerations, *"Now Bob, you know that aint the way it was"* and Guy Imus grumbling about Gertrude Bowles jokingly calling him Mr. Eemus, trumping her with *"and good day to you Mrs. Bowels."*

One of my first memories of Curt was how large he looked in the small log cabin at the homestead. His large frame dominated the room. He had to duck down a little to go through the doorway into the kitchen. The ceiling was low and Curt (and Granddad) seemed to fill the room. Whenever we visited the homestead, Curt was there, at least for mealtime. When all seven of us sat down for a meal in the kitchen, it was a full house. Curt, Granddad and my father always had a lot to talk about. Stories about engines, sawmills, hunting, trapping and prospecting ensued. Granddad was loud, and the livelier the conversation got, the louder he got; Curt used a lot of emphasis when he talked, so before long, someone had to tone it down a little. Curt's wife, Beryl, had a pretty commanding voice of her own, so when she spoke, everyone took notice. She was never one to hold back with the expletives either, so after her little tirade, everybody had a good laugh and took a breather. Mealtime in the old cabin is where I learned the art of tipping your chair back—balancing on the back two legs to create a rocking chair effect. All the men did it, usually after the meal when they lit up a smoke and needed a sitting-down-stretch. It was terribly hard on the chairs, and the attic over the porch was littered with broken chair parts waiting for repair, which usually meant screws, glue and lots of hay wire criss-crossed between the legs where the rungs attached. I don't think I ever saw a chair at the old place without those modifications.

Curt was born September 5, 1915 at Chelan Falls, Washington, to Hugh and Mamie Courtney. The family had been working various jobs around the lower end of the lake when, in the spring of 1917, Hugh took a job at Stehekin working at the Lesh sawmill five miles up the Stehekin Valley, on the south side of the Stehekin River. Thus began the life of the Hugh Courtney family in Stehekin. The spring of 1918 found them moving to the abandoned McComb

Young Curt at the homestead about 1919

June, Ray and Curt at Stehekin Landing about 1929.
Unknown girl on the left.

homestead about a mile-and-a-half upriver from the Lesh property, where Curt grew up, learning a life in the mountains.

Curt, his older brother Laurence, and their two older half-siblings, Dorothy and Harwood Lotspiech, found plenty to do around the homestead, but Mamie kept a close eye on them. The woods were like a dark jungle right up close to the cabin. Huge fir trees, some as high as 150 feet, surrounded the entire area like giant statues. Mamie was always afraid the kids would wander off and get eaten by a bear or fall into the roaring Stehekin River nearby. Compared to today, life on the homestead in 1918 was very basic. There were no cars; no roads other than the crude wagon trail the Courtneys carved out of the woods, no neighbors for over a mile, and a very basic, 18x20, one-room log cabin with a dirt floor. Growing up in that environment made tough, self-reliant people. Curt was no exception. He loved being around the animals, learning to use tools, leather craft, hunting, trapping and fishing. Building things was another of his passions. Anytime he and Laurence could get a few slabs of reject lumber from the Lesh mill, they hauled them home for building projects on the farm, often, something functional like a simple table or bench or a bridge over the ditch from Battalion Creek. Working with tools and lumber became second nature when living in the woods. It's what you did.

Curt and the other boys liked to go to the landing at boat time to visit and get the mail. Before they had a car, it wasn't uncommon to walk the seven miles down, hang out at the landing, get the mail and walk the seven miles back. If they were lucky, they sometimes got a ride with Harry Jamison, better known as Jamey, from Rainbow Lodge in his touring car, cutting off about three miles of walking. Occasionally, on the way home, they crossed the river at Boulder Creek to visit with friends, Bob and Doris. They walked on up the trail on that side of the river, visited their half-sister, Dorothy Byrd, at her homestead, then walked home. With any luck, they'd find the cows on the way and herd them home.

Work was a way of life on the farm, and Curt did his share of it. There was land to clear; poles to cut and peel; shakes to split for outbuilding roofs; firewood to cut; feed to haul for the animals; water to haul from the river; gardens to plow, rake and plant. The list goes on. And most of this work was done by hand. Later, when they had a gas-driven drag saw, (a powered reciprocating cross-cut saw you could drag around the woods with a horse) cutting firewood was supposedly a little easier, but according to nearly ten consecutive entries in Mom's journal, Hugh spent more time working on the drag saw than working with it.

Today, when we cut firewood, we take our truck and chainsaw, cut up the wood and haul it home. If we are on the ball and work steadily, we can finish it up in a week or two. In those days, it was quite different. Without the use of chainsaws, and only a horse or two to drag the logs close to the house, trees were felled as near the farm as possible so they could use a homemade wheelbarrow to haul the pieces to the woodshed. It was nearly a year-round process since the wood was used not only for heat, but cooking and heating water as well.

Hauling water from the river was a year round chore. Open-topped, square, five gallon lard cans with round wooden handles in the top were used. Hugh carved a yoke that sat on your shoulders with a rope on each side attached to the cans, helping take some of the weight off your arms. That way, a man could make several trips in a row with ten gallons at a time. Laundry was done almost daily,

early on with a scrub board, later with a gas-driven Maytag washing machine. A hand-operated wringer was mounted over a washtub next to the washing machine. Then, of course, they needed lots of water for bathing, which they did in one of the laundry tubs.

Curt and Ray with two Dolly Varden about 1931

Since access to the Courtney place was just a horse and wagon trail, they put up a cable trolley across the river so they could use the main road on the other side. It was only a couple of miles either way up to Mac's or down to Skinny Wilson's, and a bit easier to get a ride one way or the other. The 7/8 galvanized steel cable was attached to a large tree on the other side of the river. Guy wires held the tree rigid to keep the cable tight. On this side, since there wasn't a suitable tree where they needed it, they hung a large pulley off a stout pole set in the ground, ran the cable through that and down to a deadman, which was a fairly good size log buried in the ground at right angles to the cable. A turnbuckle was used for adjusting the cable tight. Elevated platforms and ramps were added at each end and a lightweight wooden platform hanging off the cable from two sheaves served as the trolley. It carried about three people sitting down, one in front of the other. The trolley was hand-powered by pulling yourself along hand-over-hand from the

The trolley at the homestead.

main cable overhead. The cardinal rule was to never let your hands go behind your head as you were pulling. If you did, they could be run over by the back sheave. The first half of the ride was easy since the weight of the load created more sag in the line the further out you got, giving you a downhill ride. Once you reached the center of the cable, it was uphill the rest of the way. The tighter the cable, the straighter it was, thus less sag and not as much work pulling yourself up the second half. One time, when Curt was going across, the deadman pulled part way out of the ground, letting the cable sag to the point where the trolley was in the water. After a considerable amount of yelling for someone to help him, Laurence came out with a rope and between the two of them, managed to pull Curt and the trolley up the steep incline to safety.

I was about eleven the first time I got to use the trolley by myself. It was a huge deal! I was excited and scared at the same time. Would I make it without losing all my fingers in the sheaves? Would I be strong enough to haul myself up the other side? What would happen if I couldn't? Well, it all worked out and after that I was out there on the thing all the time. I always had some excuse to go across to the other side. A couple of my more memorable trips come to mind. One time I went over to explore the area across the road, just above what is now the Bowles's place at about six-and-a-half miles. I got close to a den of rattlesnakes while climbing through some dense brush. It didn't take long to get out of there and back across to the safe side. The other time, I took my newly acquired 22 rifle over to hunt grouse. Granddad offered to cook them up for dinner that night if I got any. He also gave me a few clues where to look for them. Sure enough, I got two while standing behind the double fir trees right along the road. After getting back across the river, Granddad taught me how to clean and cook them in a breaded batter just like fried chicken. What a treat that was.

Curt and Beans in front of the barn

Having a car in the family dramatically changed how they lived. Not only did the maintenance on the vehicle become another chore, but constantly working on the road between the Leshes and the homestead also kept them busy. The Forest Service never really recognized the upper Company Creek Road, so maintenance and snow removal was pretty much up to the Courtneys. They couldn't do much about snow removal other than shoveling out places in the spring that were slow to melt. They spent many days doing just that. Getting the road open that time of year was an important part of their existence. Once open, they could haul feed, supplies, repair parts and building materials much more easily than taking things across the trolley. Working on the road bed itself was always a work in progress, repairing flood damage, removing down trees, hauling dirt with a wheelbarrow and constantly digging rocks out of the road, all by hand. It took a lot of time, but it was just the way things worked back then. Hugh and the boys did most of the road

work, but June and Mamie got their share of it as well. Sometimes, Bob Boehm, Skinny Wilson's stepson, also helped. He and the boys spent a lot of time together, so it was natural for him to help out. After the road was snow-free and repaired, Curt and Laurence kept pretty busy hauling different family members around the valley. An entry from June's journal dated Saturday, June 23, 1934 reads in part:

"...Laurence came home this morning at ten o'clock. About eleven o'clock they went to the boat. They waited for Curtice, he came up from Lucerne in a motorboat, and they all got home at two fifteen. Just a little while after they got here, Dad called up from the road camp and wanted someone to go down to get him. Curtice went down and they got back at three thirty. We had dinner then. Dad came down from Boulder Creek camp."

Curt by Hugh's 1922 Dodge

Over the next six years, Curt worked on a number of jobs between Holden Mine and Stehekin. During apple harvests he usually worked for the Buckners, picking apples and other orchard duties. He worked quite a bit for Jack Blankenship, running folks up to fishing camps, and general handyman work at the landing. He worked for several other people around the valley on a variety of short-term jobs—hauling rock and brick for the Wilsons, road work for the Forest Service, milking cows for Mack, and helping Dorothy out down on her place. Of course, there always was plenty to do around the homestead, which included helping Ray get logs and cut shakes for his cabin, building a barrel stove for a heater in the cabin (the same stove Nancy and I have been using in our house since 1972), cutting wood, clearing land, keeping the sawmill running, and a host of other chores. He worked at least a year at Holden mine as a laborer helping build the dormitories, mess hall, and reduction mill in preparation for getting the mine into production.

In December 1941, shortly after the bombing of Pearl Harbor, Curt was drafted into the army and attended basic training at Camp Roberts, California. When I first started researching his military service, I had no idea what to expect. I knew he worked with mules, mostly in the mountain troops, and spent a few months on Kiska Island in the Aleutian chain of Alaska. That was about it. I remembered, back in the 1970s, finding his uniform down in the old cabin stored in the bottom of a wooden bolt box with the words Bethlehem Steel Company stenciled on the top. Fast forward to 2009, when I dug out the uniform and decided to take a closer look. Inside one of the pockets was a wallet, filled with wartime pictures, liberty passes, addresses, gas ration stamps and more. It was like he just took it off yesterday. Everything was in such good condition, I couldn't believe it. Folded for sixty-five years was a

Curt in Mamie's garden. ca.1941

piece of lined notebook paper with a girl's address on it. There was a photo of Curt sitting in the berry patch at home—one he asked Mamie to send him so he could give it to his girl near Camp Hale in 1943. That snapshot somehow stayed in his wallet. A cartoon of Hitler standing in front of a fortune teller, digging in his pocket for a dollar, and the psychic telling him "no charge…your future isn't worth a dollar." These items and other pieces of memorabilia sparked my interest in knowing more about his time in the army. What I found later in some of my mother's things completed the puzzle. There were several neatly tied bundles of letters written by Curt to Hugh and Mamie during his military service—late 1941 through most of 1944. After reading all of them, I got to know Curt in a way I had not known him.

While still in basic training, Curt's skills in mountain life and with animals were sought after by the cadre looking for men to be assigned to the new 87th Mountain Infantry Regiment at Fort Lewis, Washington, also known as the Ski Patrol. This unit was made up of world-class mountaineers, skiers, lumbermen, muleskinners, horsemen, forest rangers, guides, cowboys and regular army cadre. Skiing and training in the mountains of Washington, close to home, suited him fine. He was getting along fine in the army but clearly, like so many of the men, his thoughts were always of home.

He wrote letters to the family on a regular schedule of Sunday, Tuesday and Thursday so they would arrive in Stehekin to coincide with the three-day boat schedule of Monday, Wednesday and Friday. That way, Hugh and Mamie received mail from him every boat day. A letter dated April 5, 1942 reads in part…

"Dearest Folks,
Well, here I am again for a few lines to let you know that I am OK and feel good. How are you folks getting along and feeling these days? Well, what is everybody doing around over there now days? Is the snow about all gone yet? I suppose it is by now. How are Dad and Ray getting along with all of their work? Well, my work don't ever seem to change any at all here, but it is not too bad and is the best I have found in the army yet. Boy, you should see all the clothes I have got now. Of course it is all winter stuff but sure is good. Ray sure would like the kind of ski shoes and skis we have I'll bet. And, we have got a sleeping bag that is a mummy, what I mean, they cost $10 more than Ray thought they did so you can see from that what kind of a bag they must be. They say we can sleep right out in the snow with them at 70 below and not be cold at all, but I hope I never have to though. I don't want to give them that test. I will take their word for it. Did you folks have a nice Easter Sunday? I suppose you and Dad went out to see if you could find some Rabbit eggs this morning, didn't you? Oh, sure! I got up too late myself – everyone else had got them. Well, you folks be careful now, all of you all the time and so will I.
So, till next time, your loving son and bro, Curt."

Every letter ended with the same sentence about being careful. Curt knew how hard the work was on the farm and how hard it was on Hugh and Mamie. At fifty-six years old, their bodies were wearing down. His deep concern for their safety and welfare was apparent and he did everything he could, sometimes just with words, to make life better for them.

It was just a matter of time until Ray was drafted, leaving Hugh and Mamie alone to take care of all the work at home. My grandparents both had medical issues limiting the amount of work they could do. Laurence worked at the Holden mine contributing money on a regular basis but not getting much time off to help, and my mother and father lived in Wenatchee. Curt started talking to his captain about getting a hardship leave to go home and help out in the mill. Hugh had timber orders from Holden mine but needed help running the mill. Curt never had much luck getting a block of time off, but my dad was able to get some hardship time off from his defense- related job in Wenatchee. He and Mom and my older sister, Mary, moved to Stehekin for the summer of 1942 to help out.

Another of Curt's pursuits in the army was to get Ray into the same outfit with him. He figured, since Ray was going to get drafted anyway, maybe he should join for the mountain troops. Curt started sending Ray information about it and putting in a good word for him every chance he got. He figured Ray's knowledge about skiing, horse packing and other mountaineering skills would more than qualify him for the outfit, possibly even getting him into officers' school.

As spring turned into summer, the men in Curt's outfit hung up the skis and started working with mules. Each man was assigned

Curt, third from left, with army buddies at Camp Roberts, CA.

a mule to feed, train and take care of. That was his job. Curt liked this duty as well and in a note home spoke about his mule.

"...I like to see what I can teach that mule of mine and every day I work on him a little bit and he seems to learn fast too. He is kind of a simple old thing – looks like he is always smiling but I don't think he is though. I am teaching him to shake hands now and if I do it every day, he don't forget, but if I miss one day, I have to get him started for the first time but he will make it alright. I have got him so he comes to me when I call him. It took him awhile to get used to it but he learned after awhile."

Curt compared working with the mules as more like being on a farm than in the army. And on the farm is where his heart and mind was. In almost every letter home he asks about the sawmill, garden, animals and Mamie's cooking, usually in that order. As long as I can remember, Curt has been involved with sawmills, talking about them all the time. Now I see the fascination began at an early age. Even in the army, when he had free time, he always looked for parts and engines to make things better at the mill at home.

In June of 1942, Ray entered the army and after basic training at Camp Roberts, was assigned to the 87th Infantry Mountain Regiment with Curt at Ft. Lewis. Curt's efforts to get Ray into the regiment paid off, though it wasn't long before the outfit was shipped to Hunter-Liggett Military Reservation near Jolon, California for maneuvers. By this time, Curt had switched jobs from a mule skinner to stable hand, a job he liked even better, since he rarely had to go out on the daily hikes and stable hands lived away from the main garrison, close to the mules. That suited him fine since he got pretty annoyed with all the noise in the barracks. His job there included leatherwork, taking care of the saddles and gear and other general stable duties. By December of that year, they were on the move again. This time a scenic train ride took them to Camp Hale, Colorado, a brand new camp on the Continental Divide at 9,480 feet elevation, designed for sub-zero testing of all kinds of military equipment. Curt mentioned in a letter home that it got down to thirty-six below zero one night but it still felt warmer than the mountains of California. Shortly after their arrival, he and Ray were out on skis having the time of their lives. The dry snow was the best they had ever seen.

On June 11, 1943, the outfit moved to Fort Ord, California for amphibious training in preparation for combat operations. Nobody knew where they were heading, but it certainly looked like they were finally going to see combat. They had been training

Curt running the carriage in Ray and Vigil's sawmill.

for well over a year now, and the rumors were abundant about where they were going. It didn't take long to find out. By the end of July, they were part of Amphibious Technical Force Nine on their way to Kiska Island in the Aleutian Islands. The Japanese had occupied Kiska but fortunately got word of the large task force and pulled out before they arrived, leaving all their equipment behind. Curt was popular with the officers shortly after landing on Kiska by taking generators and batteries off Japanese trucks and hooking them all up together on one vehicle to make a lighting system for the officers' tents. His life on the farm taught him how to be creative and make do with what you have, a skill that served him well in the army.

After Ray was drafted in 1942, Curt again started working on ways to get out on a hardship discharge because of all the work left with Hugh and Mamie. He never gave up. Nearly every letter home had some mention of it, asking Hugh to solicit and write letters to his commanding officer expressing the need for him to be home to run the sawmill, their only source of income. Hugh gathered letters from local businesses, including the Boat Company and Holden Mine (the mine was supplying copper to the military and needed the timbers that the Courtney sawmill had contracted to cut), and sent them off. Thanks to the Red Cross, the slow wheels of the army started to turn in Curt's favor, but it would be several months before final action was taken.

In December of 1943, Curt and Ray, along with the rest of the outfit, were sent back to the states—this time to Camp Carson, Colorado. From here the two brothers were separated. In February of 1944, Curt's Battalion joined the 10th Light Division and moved back to Camp Hale. Ray was assigned to the 90th Infantry and stayed at Camp Carson for the time being. In Camp Hale, Curt put in for a packing job with the mules and in March of 1944, he was transferred to the 257th Quartermaster Pack Company and later became a saddler with that company, a job he particularly liked because, as he said, *"Whenever we go into the field on maneuvers, I have a mule to ride, and that sure beats walking."*

Curt in army uniform with Beans at the homestead.

Curt in the Aleutian Islands with Japanese truck and lighting system he developed.

Meanwhile, Curt made progress on his application for discharge. He was interviewed by a colonel and told that it sounded like a sure thing to him. They were just waiting for word from Washington D.C. and if it passed there, then the last stop was the local draft board in Wenatchee, Washington. They had the final say in the matter. About this time, Curt started having pretty serious back and leg problems. It got to the point he could hardly work and from time to time was admitted to the hospital, but they couldn't really find anything wrong. While in the hospital one time, he met a fellow from Montana, and they got to talking about home and fishing. The Montana guy told Curt that salmon eggs weren't allowed as bait in Montana, but they surely were the best way to catch fish. The guy's brother, still living in Montana, would do just about anything for a supply of salmon eggs. Never to pass up an opportunity to make a few bucks, Curt suggested that maybe he could get his dad to send the brother a supply of eggs and in turn could make a few dollars to help out at home. Sure enough, a deal was struck and Hugh packaged up twelve bottles of eggs and sent them to the brother, while Curt collected the money from his friend in the hospital and mailed it on to Hugh. This was typical of Curt's style all his life; he never ceased making deals, although some didn't always pan out as well as the salmon egg venture, and usually the stakes were much higher with considerable risks involved.

In June of 1944, Curt's battalion made what was to become his last major move in the army. They joined up with the 87th Infantry Regiment Light, moving to Camp Swift, Texas to join up with the new 10th Mountain Division. Unknown to Curt at the time, the 10th was gearing up to sail to Naples, Italy and consequently was involved in heavy fighting. Many of his old friends were killed in this action. But for Curt, it wasn't in the cards to go. After his

Laurence and Curt and Beans the dog at the homestead ca. 1933

McConnell cabin.

Chelan resident who had a summer cabin near where Stehekin Pastry Company stands today. An avid fisherman, Lon spent as much time here in the valley as possible, fishing the upper end of the lake with his pals, Helen and Paul Kinzel.

Paul Kinzel and Lon Varney with a nice catch at Stehekin.

back trouble started, the paper work finally came through, and his discharge was approved. In November of 1944, he was finally on his way home, six weeks before the outfit boarded the ship to Europe.

Back home in Stehekin, Curt's post-war plans were starting to come together. Hugh and Mamie were thrilled to have at least one son home, out of harm's way and to help out on the farm. The winter of 1944 – '45 turned out to be a very mild one, so work on outdoor projects continued almost without interruption. The greatest snow depth measured at Buckners' orchard was nine inches, not bad when the average was six or seven feet. Curt went back to work on his cabin near the upper property line of the homestead. Jane and Grant McConnell were in the process of buying the cabin. They planned to move in as soon as Grant was discharged from the Navy, which turned out to be December of 1945. In the summer of 1944, while still in the Army, Curt hired Lon Varney to build a rock fireplace on the downvalley end of the cabin. Lon was a

Curt and Hugh, with the help of Laurence, continued to run the sawmill and work on the new house for Mamie. Curt and Laurence also finished up projects on the McConnell place, developing a water system from the spring behind the house and putting in a real bathroom with toilet, sink and shower, pretty modern for those days. When Jane and Grant arrived in December 1945, the fire was going and Laurence had kept the road open with his car in order to haul up their gear and groceries—a warm welcome if there ever was one. They were lucky to get here when they did. On January 24 a huge snowstorm dumped two feet of new snow overnight, bringing the total on the ground to fifty-seven inches. Colder nighttime temperatures allowed for great skiing, and it wasn't long before Curt, Ray, and the Buckner girls and others were organizing a two-day ski party at their new neighbors' cabin. Having no time to resist, the McConnell's opened their house to one and all. Food and drink was packed in and a large bonfire built, thus continuing the trend of valley ski parties at different homes throughout the community.

Over the next several years, Curt worked on a number of projects around the valley. The sawmill took priority over everything since it was needed to make lumber for his other passion—building houses. But getting timber was starting to be a problem. Most of the good trees on the homestead were already cut, other than thirty or so around the house and barn that Mamie wanted to keep. Timber sales from the Forest Service were increasingly harder to get since the government wanted to do large sales that required bidding. The Courtneys were in no position to take on sales of that size. Though they managed to get a few trees to stockpile enough lumber for two or three houses, the mill slowly went out of business.

Frank Lesh, Hugh Courtney, Laurence in driver's seat and Curt with a load of logs on an army scout car at the homestead.

School work party re-opening the school after being closed for nine years. Front row left to right: Dad Imus, Deke Wheeler, Virgil Fellows, Guy Imus, unknown. Back row left to right: Tony Sargo, Ray Courtney, Bob Dunkin, Grant McConnell, Albert Lent, Hugh Courtney, Pete Miller. ca. 1948

Chelan County had recently acquired the Stehekin road system from the Forest Service, and needing men to work year-round, hired Curt for the newly created position of foreman. Curt saw an opportunity and before long, he purchased a Caterpillar grader and D-7 dozer which he rented back to the county. One of the unwritten requirements for getting a job on the road was having school-age children. The school had closed nine years earlier for lack of students. Curt held the key for not only keeping the road open but for getting the school started back up as well. He also needed men to build houses for the families to live in. One of the first to move to the valley was the Lewis Pickering family from Oroville, Washington. Lew was Curt's sergeant most of the time while in the army. They became good friends, and Curt always talked about Stehekin with his friends. Lew and his wife had three school-age children, which suited Curt just fine. He and Laurence built a nice, rustic cabin near the river for the Pickerings about three hundred yards upvalley from the home place. Building near the river was more of a necessity than for aesthetic purposes, since water had to be carried from the river unless you were fortunate enough to have a creek or spring nearby.

In the summer of 1948, a potluck work party took place at the school near Rainbow Falls in preparation for re-opening the school that fall. It was a large gathering, and many of the old-timers, as well as newcomers, came to help out. Paul Bergman, the local photographer, took a picture of the work party posed next to the upvalley side of the school. Curt's plan was coming together.

The next big event in Curt's life came in 1950 when he and Beryl Imus Blankenship were married. Beryl was the widow of Jack Blankenship, who died the summer of 1949. Beryl and Jack were the owners of the café, rooming house and post office at the landing. Curt was familiar with the operation at the landing, having worked off and on for Jack over several years. After Jack died, Curt continued helping Beryl out. The union worked well. Beryl had already established herself as a fine cook and cordial hostess. On the other hand, Curt had the knowledge and creativity to expand on what Jack and Beryl had already started. What Curt lacked in business sense, he made up for with ambition. Beryl's skills with finance and budgeting kept Curt's dreams and sometimes-outlandish ideas mostly within the budget. I remember staying with them a couple of times in the winters around 1959. They were in the new house by then. Granddad sat at his desk in one corner of the living room, and Curt sat in the new radio corner at the other end. Beryl was either in the kitchen or sitting on the couch facing the fireplace reading a book. Curt was listening to a favorite radio program, sketching and scribbling in a notebook at the same time. His mind was always working, even when listening to the radio. Periodically, he would get out his tape measure from a drawer in the desk and pull out a few inches of tape, studying and calculating numbers, inches and feet. When the punch line to a particularly funny skit was coming, he would stop what he was doing, look over at you, smile with that look of anticipation and just at the right moment of climax, would do a little thing with his arms as if directing an orchestra (a little trait he picked up from Granddad), then go back to doodling in his notebook. He clearly enjoyed sitting there on those winter evenings making plans, with the fire roaring and snow falling outside.

In the late summer of 1950, Curt and Beryl added a new dining room and tavern on the north side of the log lunch counter, more than doubling the seating capacity of the café. Additionally, they landscaped and paved a large patio area on the west side of the additions, providing out-door seating overlooking the lake. During

Stehekin Landing about 1952. Morse's Resort jeep on the left next to Golden West Lodge pick-up, and on the right Andy's Taxi. Daisy Weaver and Dad Imus standing next to the pick-up with backs to the camera on the far right.

Hugh Courtney at his desk in the new house, about 1960.

U-Drive car rental and Curt and Beryl's.

Beryl and Curt Courtney, Lemerne Sullivan, Echo and Chuck Clayson in the coffee shop.

the summer months, locals and tourists alike enjoyed the pleasant atmosphere. Curt and Beryl had a genuine talent for making people feel special and welcome at their establishment. Everyone who walked through the door was greeted as an old friend. Soon, the word got out, and local folks from Chelan, Wenatchee, and beyond were making the trip to Stehekin, not only for the adventure of the lake and mountains but to spend time with Curt and Beryl and enjoy Beryl's famous Washington Nut Pie. In 1955, they sold one-third interest in the landing property to Bill and Lemerne Sullivan. The Sullivans, along with their twins Betty and Billy, moved into the apartment above the café. After a couple of years, not liking the solitude of the winters, Bill moved back to Seattle. Curt, Beryl and Lemerne continued to run the business.

The summer of 1960 saw significant changes coming to the valley. Maurice Kerr, owner of Silver Bay, headed up a petition to Chelan County PUD to study the feasibility of providing electricity to Stehekin. Most everyone living in the valley filled out a form indicating what electric appliances they would like to have. Washing machines, water pumps, refrigerators and freezers topped the list. After several options were discussed, one of which was extending the old Holden Mine power line up the lake from Prince Creek, they entered into an agreement with Art Peterson to use his already-installed pipeline from Company Creek and a small hydro turbine he had in place. Little did they know that the line from Prince Creek would have been by far the cheaper and most efficient option. As it turned out, the pipeline and intake needed extensive work, and cavitation problems on unstable ground caused many outages from breakdowns and repairs on the hydro plant. By 1966, a contract was let to Cusick's Construction of Wenatchee to build a new pipeline and powerhouse a little further up the road just across Company Creek.

But let's back up to 1962 when bidding took place for right-of-way clearing and installation of nine miles of transmission line in the valley. Five bids were received, two of which were from L.D. Kiethly and Curt Courtney. L.D., the owner of the Golden West Lodge, was also Curt's competitor in the food and lodging business. Because the Golden West was up the hill away from the landing, and Curt and Beryl's was front and center at the boat landing, the Kiethlys had to be creative with ways to get folks to eat and stay at their lodge instead of the landing. It seems like every time they added another sign at the road going up the hill, Curt would do something to counter that, like park his open air Rainbow Falls bus

Paul Bergman walking up the hill to the Golden West Lodge. Photo courtesy The Wenatchee World.

Curt in his Rainbow Falls bus at Stehekin Landing. Lady of the Lake on the left, Speedway on the right.

just a little closer to the gang plank, or paint a bigger sign on the back of the bus. Their rivalry was apparent, and if Curt didn't like someone, he would just glare at him. As jovial and friendly as Curt was, he didn't like competition, and it was written all over his face. It just about drove him crazy to have someone trying to outdo him on the home court. It started coming to a head when L.D. put up a set of loud speakers by the large sign over the Golden West road at the landing. As the boat pulled in, loud music started playing, much like what you hear at a circus. Then, Mr. Kiethly's voice came on over the music, describing what the lodge had to offer. To the tourists getting off the boat, it sounded like entering the big top, as the elephants and lions and everything else were running around in a circle, loudspeakers blaring. Clearly, that scene wasn't helping anyone at Stehekin. It became a battle between two men, having very little to do with providing a pleasant experience for the visitor.

In September 1962, Chelan County PUD accepted the low bid of $27,018.00 submitted by Mr. Kiethly. That didn't help the already strained relationship between the two men, but in the long run, Curt came out okay. When the job was mostly finished, Curt contracted the cleanup of the huge piles of logs located around the valley. He salvaged many logs for lumber, while also selling a great deal of it for firewood. And he had one more ace up his sleeve.

Until 1963, the only lodging provided at Curt and Beryl's was a couple of rooms at the Whitehouse, a white, two story building on the downlake side of the café. The main level housed Paul Bergman's photo shop and later, the post office, after it was moved from a very small porch-like addition at the café. In the fall of that year, they tore the Whitehouse down and started building a new, thirty-two by eighty, three-story facility called the Boatel, providing extra space in the back for the kitchen, freezers, storage,

Curt in front of the White House.

The new Boatel, where the White House once stood at Stehekin Landing.

and making pies. Paul's Photoshop, Buckner's Store and the Post Office occupied the front of the building, while an apartment for Curt and Beryl sat right behind the photo shop. Curt and Beryl moved down to the landing in the early summer and back home after the season was over, eliminating the fourteen-mile round-trip drive from the homestead every day. The second story offered a lobby in front overlooking the lake and eight modern rooms complete with full baths and heat. The back of the building had a third story called the penthouse—a nice, fully equipped two-bedroom apartment. Lemerne continued living in the apartment above the café in the summers but moved into the penthouse during the winter providing limited lunch services mostly for locals at boat time.

Curt stayed in touch daily with Granddad over the old crank phone. I happened to be with Hugh a few times when Curt called, always around 5:30 pm during dinner. Whenever the phone rang, you had to wait and see if it was your ring. A long, two shorts and a long was Granddad's ring. He would do the same orchestra-directing thing as Curt did with the radio program, only using one hand sometimes. Everything stopped when the phone was ringing. No talking was allowed. It was like you didn't exist. If it wasn't his ring, he'd look at his watch and start wondering aloud where Curt was. But of course Curt couldn't call if someone else was on the line. The only way to tell if the line was open was to lift the receiver off the hook and listen, but the clicking sound this made could be heard by the party talking. Some folks around the valley liked to listen just to keep up on the gossip, especially since everyone knew each other's ring. It was easy to select who you wanted to listen to, but no matter how gently the receiver was lifted and replaced, it still made a noise. More than once Guy Imus scolded the offending culprit…by name. When that happened, the person

rubber-necking slammed the receiver down hard, not bothering to try and hide the sound. It was a guess, of course, as to who was listening, but I think they were usually right. The two people most responsible had gained a reputation around the valley. The phone also helped Donald Rice keep track of time. He liked to call Granddad and ask what time it was or what day it was or if it was a boat day. He never signed off or said goodbye, just abruptly hung up, sometimes talking to himself as the line went dead.

Donald Rice at the landing.

Like a lot of us in Stehekin, Curt was a collector. He especially liked finely-crafted hand tools. I remember helping him move some things at the new house and noticed, on the headboard corner post of his bed, a nice leather tool holder full of new, brightly colored, plastic-handled screwdrivers (he used to call them glass-handled). I made a comment about how nice they were, and he just beamed. You could tell how proud he was of that collection. But, to my surprise, the bedpost was their permanent home, not just a place to hang the tool holder while we were working, and I suspected those tools weren't to be used, only admired, like a restored car in a museum. I often wondered how many women have husbands with a nice collection of screwdrivers hanging from the corner of the bed. But it wasn't just screwdrivers. A pine cabinet with a dozen small drawers for holding little screws and parts had the same effect. He once bought a large, old warehouse down in Ocean Park, Washington, stocked with cases of brand new half-pint jars used for canning oysters. The jars were nice, but there weren't any lids, just boxes of squeaky-clean, glass jars. I can hear his words today: *"Here, take a case or two of these home to Nancy. I'm sure she can use them."* The slightest hint that you may not want them would suggest that you didn't like his jars. It was much easier to take them and agree, *"Yes, I'm sure she can."* I think all of my cousins, and probably anyone else that took a tour of the warehouse, walked out with oyster jars to take home to their wives.

I never tired of listening to Curt's stories and his interest in so many things. After just a few minutes, you couldn't help but feel that same exuberance for whatever he was talking about. It was contagious. He once told me about taking a tour of a factory in Seattle that made large gears and shafts for ocean-going ships. Those five-ton gears exited him as much as the little oyster jars. To him, it was all the same neat stuff.

Stehekin Landing about 1945

Curt in front of his bus at Stehekin Landing.

Throughout the 1960s, Stehekin Landing, as the business was now called, continued to grow. Curt's small rental car fleet grew to about a dozen cars, mostly 1951 Chevrolets. It made economical sense to have the same kind of vehicles when repairs were needed, and those old Chevys were quite simple to work on. He hired a mechanic to run his shop up near Boulder Creek; he not only worked on Curt's vehicles but most everyone else's in the valley as well. The mechanic, Ed Leaf, was a familiar face to us all. An older man, he knew all the tricks of old school, back-yard mechanics as well as the more technical complete engine rebuild. Ed was a welcome addition to the valley. Rarely staying over the winter, he built a small summer cabin on part of the old Frank Lesh homestead about two miles up Company Creek Road, called, of course, The Leaf House.

As the debate for creating the North Cascades National Park heated up in the late 1960s, a cloud of uncertainty settled over the valley. Residents and landowners didn't know what to expect. Early maps outlining the proposed Park included Stehekin within the boundaries. Rumors and speculations ran high as concerns mounted about what would become of Stehekin. Deep-rooted old timers were especially upset, fearing they may have to leave not only their homes, but also a way of life.

Curt, after living in Stehekin nearly fifty years, felt those concerns like a knife in his side. He was a central figure in just about everything that went on in the valley. Whether it was the landing, roads, building houses, or buying and selling property, Curt was involved. The threat of all that changing came down hard on Curt. It was the only life he knew, and he knew it well. As congressional hearings wrapped up and maps were redrawn, it was decided the Stehekin Valley would be left out of the Park proper but included in what was to be called The Lake Chelan National Recreation Area, managed by the National Park Service. The National Park boundary was established at High Bridge, eleven miles up the Stehekin River. The bill was passed in late summer, 1968. Stehekin was about to enter one of the most trying periods of its one hundred-year history.

Over the next eighteen months, Curt, Beryl and Lemerne continued to operate the Stehekin Landing, but clearly, the National Park wanted to buy the facility. It became increasingly difficult for Curt to deal with the bureaucracy. Negotiations were under way for the transfer of the roads from the county to the park, leaving Curt without control. He could tell his days were numbered for living in the valley he once described in a letter as, *"The only place in the world I want to live. Stehekin has everything a man could ever want."* He found out that it had a little more than a man could want. The spring of 1970 saw the end of an era. Curt and Beryl signed papers with the National Park Service, officially terminating private ownership of the landing. The Courtneys bought property down on the Long Beach Peninsula in Ocean Park, Washington, where they soon became involved in a new life. But before they could start seriously moving all of Curt's stuff, he had to build a large shop to have a place to put everything. Dennis Lund and I worked for Curt helping build the shop and driving the many trips, which involved loading the trucks in Stehekin, shipping them out on the barge to Chelan and driving to Ocean Park—about a six-hour drive depending which truck you drove. He had two—one, a fairly comfortable and powerful two-ton flatbed Chevrolet. The other was an old underpowered four-speed moving van of 1950s vintage. The van took eight hours. Every hill was agonizingly slow, causing traffic to back up, even in the right-hand slow lane. I remember pulling into State Patrol weigh stations, surrounded by forty-foot eighteen-wheelers and wanting to crawl in a hole! One of Curt's bargain buys didn't help my ego in those situations and, on top of that, he half-jokingly asked why it took so much longer with the van. I asked him to come along sometime and I'd show him, but he never took me up on it, knowing full well what the problem was. Defeat didn't come easy for Curt.

Relocating to Ocean Park had its pitfalls. Curt was the new guy in town, and a small town at that. Dealing with a well-established circle of contractors and county officials, he soon learned how his old life in Stehekin looked from the other side of the table. It reminded me of the time when, back in the early 1960s, the Winkel Brothers came to Stehekin with a loader and a couple of dump trucks to get into the construction business, essentially going into competition with Curt. He didn't take it lightly, new guys coming to town and stepping on his turf. Now, he was the new guy and sometimes things didn't go like he wanted. Wading through miles of red tape to build houses and put in an RV park turned into a nightmare. His naiveté and willingness to trust everyone cost him dearly in a couple of business deals. In Chelan County, he knew people and how to get things done. One can imagine the frustrations he felt starting over and learning to play a new game, occasionally, against a stacked deck.

In 1991, after twenty years in Ocean Park, Curt and Beryl sold everything and moved to Chelan, Washington, closer to home. Even at seventy-six years old, Curt became involved in several entrepreneurial ventures, with limited success. He and Beryl also spent more time in Stehekin. With the help of several of us nephews, they built a new summer home on the back of my cousin Cragg's place. About this time, Cragg was preparing to build a large, 35x80 foot shop building, something Curt helped design

Curt and others at Beryl's graveside service in Chelan, February 1993

and build. He simply loved building, especially shops, where he liked to put a nice, partitioned room at one end with a desk and lots of drawers and cabinets for all the special stuff, while the rest of the building would be used for mechanical work on cars, trucks and heavy equipment. Summers in Stehekin suited Curt and Beryl perfectly but, unfortunately, Beryl, seven years older than Curt, started having health issues, forcing them to spend more time downlake in Chelan. On February 17, 1993, Beryl passed away from pneumonia and other related complications, leaving Curt alone for the first time in forty-three years.

While Curt was very competent in many ways, domestic chores weren't his strong suit. He didn't know a thing about cooking and household chores. Beryl's good cooking spoiled him. Meals were

Lloyd Bell and Curt at a community meeting.

always right on time and prepared to meet Curt's finicky tastes. Hamburger was the only red meat he would eat, and it had to be disguised to look like something else, like fried chicken or fish. He used to say "I don't eat meat" as if hamburger wasn't meat. Those little quirks started when he was a child. Mamie, while cooking a regular meal for the rest of the family, often had to cook a special meal for Curt. I never really knew what that was all about, but it went on for the rest of his life. Since he and Beryl had no children of their own, concerns were raised about his ability to take care of himself. Fortunately, his niece, Peggy Ann Courtney, lived in Chelan and took on the responsibility. She moved in with Curt for a period of time helping him readjust. Other good friends and relatives were quick to rise to the occasion. Peggy Ann spoke of the times when Brun Garfoot would stop by with a full case of Costco extra-creamy macaroni and cheese, by far Curt's most favorite food. Brun brought a case every time he came through town, and if it were up to Curt, he would eat Mac and Cheese for every meal. Reminded that his diabetes wouldn't support that many carbohydrates in a day, Curt proceeded to let Peggy Ann know that he knew more about what was good for him than the doctors, but in the end, he grudgingly took her advice. Meeting friends or family for coffee at his second home, the Apple Cup Café, kept routine in his life. He enjoyed the daily visits, jokingly bantering back and forth with the waitresses by means of his charming, yet sometimes crude sense of humor.

Curt loved animals, especially dogs. He and Beryl always had at least one, usually some type of little poodle. They both talked baby talk to them—something we all do—but after Beryl died, his affection towards *"Sunny Girl"* grew stronger. He nicknamed her *"The Babes"* and often referred to her as *"little people."* When told feeding cheese and ice cream to her was not healthy, he responded

"Well, if it's good for people, it's got to be good for little people." He got a huge chuckle out of feeding the dogs, watching them eat and drink, particularly ice cream or cheese. Toward the end, Peggy Ann recalled taking Sunny Girl to visit Curt in the rest home. *"I would bring her to see him in his last days and that little creature just knew she had to hang on for him—amazing".*

The last time I saw Curt was in the fall of 2000. He was in the Wenatchee Valley Medical Center recovering from having his leg amputated due to complications from diabetes. The visit was memorable and fun. Shortly after I got there, Curt had to go to the bathroom. Not wanting the nurse to help, he asked if I would. He looked so frail, I was almost afraid to touch him, but gave it my best shot, all to no avail. His skinny little body simply did not want to get out of bed. Hearing the commotion of us laughing and wrestling around there on the bed, the nurse came in and saved the day. I was relieved, and of course Curt was too. After he came back to bed, we had a great discussion about marriage and relationships, an unusual topic for Curt, I thought, but he had good things to say and it meant a lot to me. He was a thinker and philosopher, knowing a lot about a wide range of subjects. While we were talking, I noticed his bed was flat and he was up on his elbows so I offered to crank the bed up. He agreed, but when I got to the end where the cranks usually were, all I found were three buttons with very small writing below them. I mentioned to Curt that I couldn't read the writing and didn't know which button to push. *"You better watch out,"* he said, *"or this thing will throw us both out into the parking lot."* Again, we had a good laugh over the bed and I was amazed at how his witty sense of humor shown through on an otherwise dark period of his life. Two months later on December 1, 2000 Curt passed away in Chelan.

Curt at Stehekin Valley Ranch. Photo by Laura Reiter.

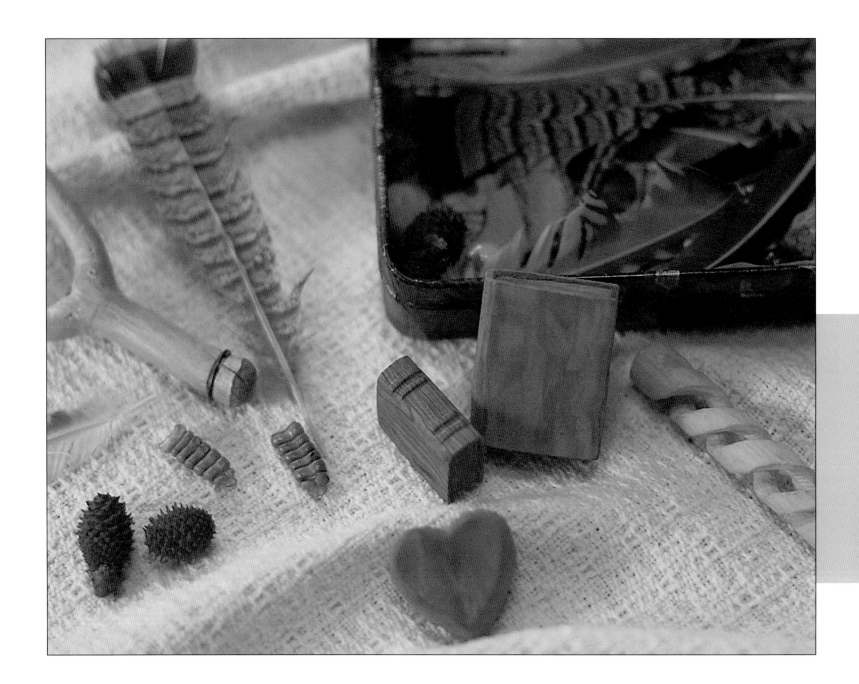

Katherine June Courtney
1918 ~ 2002

June on Digger, her favorite horse.

When I was little, growing up in Wenatchee, I used to tease my sister constantly, or anyone else for that matter. My mother, June, would sometimes get after me to knock it off, only to find me teasing her as well. She'd try to get me to stop, but I'd take off running around the outside of the house, and the chase was on. Around we'd go, me laughing and her yelling at me to stop, both of us putting on quite a show for the neighbors. Eventually, I would take a corner too fast, trip and fall, and she'd catch me. Often, if I wasn't hurt and crying, I could humor her into laughing with me. Actually, she thought it was just about as funny as I did, but it wasn't supposed to be that way!

Mike, Teddy the dog, and June Courtney Barnhart about 1950.

Born on June 16 1918, in the one-room log cabin on the Courtney homestead in Stehekin, June was the third child born to Hugh and Mamie Courtney. She grew up much the same as her brothers, helping with the chores at the homestead, where hard work was a way of life. In later years, with a gleam in her eye, she often remarked, *"It was hard work, but we always had a lot of fun."* Her journals, dating from 1933 when she was fourteen, talk of life on the farm:

Diary Starting May 10, 1933

"I was born in Stehekin on June 16, 1918. I am more nearly fifteen years of age, five feet four inches tall and weigh one hundred and fifty-eight pounds. I have brown hair, hazel eyes, and a very light complexion.

Baby June with Laurence and Curt at the homestead.

The family, including Dad, Mama, Laurence, Curtice, Ray and I live in a log cabin built forty-five years ago by a trapper. The cabin is surrounded by tall fir and pine trees.

The animals we have are Nita, the dog; Tommy, the cat; Simon, the sheep; Blue, Roney, Bridget and Brindle, the three cows and calf. Salley and Brownie, the two horses, and about a dozen chickens.

This diary is absolutely honest.

Katherine June Courtney"

"Wednesday, May 10, 1933
Weather: Cloudy and hot.
I washed the breakfast dishes and separator this morning. When I finished them I swept the floors and made two of the beds. About ten-forty-five I peeled some carrots and potatoes for dinner. After the dinner dishes were finished I studied on my high-school course until about five thirty. After supper I washed and dried the supper dishes. Today is Ray's thirteenth birthday."

"Thursday, May 11, 1933
Weather: Clear and hot this morning rained this afternoon.
Mama took care of the chickens, dried the breakfast dishes, made all of the beds, but one and washed some clothes this morning. This afternoon she rested a half an hour, did some mending and ironing, fed the chickens, and washed and dried the supper dishes.
Dad worked in the garden most of the day today. He also did a few other things.
Laurence and Curtice went down to Prince Creek after the horses today, but they did not find them. Ray went to school today. I did the general housework and mopped the front room floor this morning. This afternoon, I mopped the kitchen floor and studied. Right after supper Ray and I went after the cows, but we did not find them."

June Courtney and a calf at the homestead.

"Sunday, June 17, 1934
Weather: Clear this morning. Cloudy this P.M.
Mama did a little bit of everything today. Dad got his things ready to go out on the boat today. He is leaving Tuesday. Laurence, Curtice and Ray went after the horses this morning. They took their baths when they got back. I did the general housework this morning. This afternoon we took Curtice to the boat. (Dad and Mama stayed home.) We didn't get back until about four o'clock because we stayed at Dorothy's for a while and we had three flat tires. We took Jean and Effie (Byrd) home today. After we got home tonight Ray and I rode the horses down to the bridge. We got home at six fifteen."

"Saturday, October 20, 1934
Weather: Rained this morning. Clearing this afternoon.
Mama ironed, did some mending, mopped the kitchen floor and did a little bit of everything today. Laurence and Curtice worked on the shack and Ray made some skis. Dad and Uncle Archie worked on snow shoes and did a little bit of everything today. I did the general housework and helped with the ironing this morning. I read and took a bath this afternoon."

June's morning wake-up call was her mother Mamie, as though reading from a list, conveying to her, all the chores she had to do before walking to school. The daily task of cleaning the cream separator, involving many parts that had to be scrubbed spotless, all without running water, was June's least favorite. Mamie was especially particular about any of the food processing equipment, and inspected it like an army drill sergeant inspecting a soldier's rifle. Waking up like that was not part of the fun she mentioned earlier. She got so she hated to hear her mother's footsteps, as she knew what was in store. Mamie was a very hard worker

June at the Byrd homestead.
(National Park Service maintenance area today)

June Courtney riding Brownie near Rainbow Falls.

and expected the same from June, though whistling and telling stories did help make it fun. And, it wasn't all work and no play. When Ray was still considered "one of the little kids," he and Mom played together building forts, making little trails out in the woods, and forming a secret explorers club with the Buckner girls. The barnyard and the woods beyond were their favorite places. Mamie worried about bears out in the woods, but it was safer than playing across the road by the river. Only two years apart, they were several years younger than Laurence and Curt, and at that point in time, the big boys didn't have a lot to do with a girl and their little brother. Things changed, however, when Ray became older and more accepted by the other boys, leaving Mom home with the chores and, her best friends, the animals.

June loved working with the horses. When Hugh needed them harnessed or saddled, she always volunteered for the job, giving them a handful of oats or talking to them as she brushed their backs. Sometimes, after supper, she and Ray rode the horses bareback down to their half-sister Dorothy Byrd's place, about two-and-a-half miles away, letting them graze for a couple hours while they visited. Dorothy's husband Charley, worked away from home a lot, leaving her with three small children, as well as the animals and garden to take care of. Mom tried to help out as much as she could, sometimes staying overnight when Dorothy was sick, or bringing some of the children home to care for while Mamie and the others helped out. The two families were very close, often sharing meals and chores, and the Byrd place was a regular stop on the way to and from the landing.

Weekends at the homestead were set apart from the regular workdays. They always had a certain amount to do like feeding and watering the animals, washing dishes and getting wood and water in. For the most part, though, Saturday and Sunday were days of rest and recreation, and… bathing. Apparently, for the men anyway, baths and shaving were carried out only on weekends. June wrote in her journal several times on weekends about the men taking a bath and shaving, like it was an event worthy of writing about. Most every weekend in good weather, there was a baseball game and potluck at Keller's field, in front of what we call the Brownfield house, down by the bakery. Mom always went to the potlucks with her family, though usually not to play baseball. It was a social event, and in those days of poor roads and sometimes worse transportation, weekend socializing certainly became something to look forward to. Close in age, June and Maida Merritt were good friends, spending the night at each other's homes from time to time. The Buckner girls, Irene, Hobbie and Bucky, also were playmates, though primarily Irene since she was closer in age than the others. The Buckner swimming pool, near the ditch in the orchard, was a favorite place to play on hot summer days. On two or three occasions, Mother's Day and Fourth of July picnics were held at Bullion Camp at ten-mile, but without room for the ball games, they moved back to Keller's field, also much more centrally located in the valley.

"Sunday, May 14, 1933
Weather: Cloudy and sprinkled once in a while in the afternoon.
We all went on a picnic at Bullion today, everybody in the valley was there and three or four from Chelan. We left home about ten thirty, this morning and got home about eight forty five daylight saving time."

Maida Merritt and June Courtney

Square dances were another favorite pastime. Sometimes down at the Golden West Lodge or Buckner's, the parties would go into the wee hours of the morning. June usually went with her brothers, Laurence, Curt and Ray. All but Laurence danced. He once said, *"Dancing was an awful lot of work for what you got out of it."* Callers at the dances were usually Harry Buckner or Lon Varney. When the CCC (Civilian Conservation Corps) boys were working in the valley, square dance attendance was high, allowing for several squares. They also made the parties more interesting for Mom and the rest of the single girls.

Curt and Ray Courtney in back, June Courtney, Maida Merritt, Bucky and Hobbie Buckner in front, at the Buckner swimming pool.

After June finished the eighth grade at the Stehekin School, she started taking high school correspondence courses. Studying never came easy, but Mamie always made sure she had time set aside from chores to work on her lessons. Mom used to laughingly say, "I felt like a caged animal in school." Growing up in the woods didn't seem to allow time for formal studies. Not that she wasn't smart enough—her old school books and test sheets prove otherwise—but playing with the animals, roaming in the woods, and writing in her journal under a tall fir tree on that first patch of spring grass pulled June into the world of nature like a nail to a magnet. By the time she turned eighteen, Mom began to wonder if hard work at her parents' farm offered all there was to life. Living at the end of the road in the backwoods of Stehekin certainly didn't provide many opportunities to meet men; suitable, single men were few and far between in Stehekin. Being the only girl with three brothers, her dad, and a mother who worked like a horse, June decided it was time to leave Stehekin. It was a tough decision; she loved most everything about the valley, but she wanted to get away.

In the fall of 1936, after working a summer at the Golden West Lodge, June found a job in Chelan as a nanny, living with a family, caring for their children and doing the housework. Later she moved to Wenatchee, finding a similar job. Socializing and meeting new friends, June started to feel more comfortable with city life. One of the places she liked to go was the roller skating rink, a gathering place for many of the younger people in those days. It was there, in 1939, where she met my dad, Kenny Barnhart. Born and raised in Wenatchee, Kenny worked in the fruit industry, managing an apple orchard. About a year later, on April 12, 1940, my parents were married in Wenatchee. Their first house, on Grant Road in East Wenatchee about where Bi-Mart is today, was located in an orchard and owned by the owner of the local lumberyard. A pretty good carpenter, Dad managed to make a deal for a year's free rent in exchange for remodeling the house—a mighty good arrangement considering the country was still in the throes of the depression and wages were somewhere in the neighborhood of a dollar a day. To top it off, anytime Dad needed materials for the work, he called in the order to the landlord, and the next day, everything was delivered free of charge.

When my sister Mary was born in March 1941, my parents moved to a larger house in Wenatchee. Dad also changed jobs to Skookum growers as warehouse foreman and could walk from their new location to work. Mom took in sewing to supplement their income. Frugal living was the only way to get ahead. In 1942, after Curt and Ray were drafted in the army, Mom and Dad moved to Stehekin for the summer to help with the farm chores. June was glad to be back but the hard work never ceased. It was simply too much for her aging parents to handle. Unfortunately, my parents had to go back to Wenatchee to Dad's job for the winter. Once again the following summer they moved to Stehekin, but for a shorter time. Dad was stretching his luck taking time off. It was nice they could help out, but to stay in good graces with the draft board, he could only get so much time off.

While still in Stehekin in late summer 1943, my mother again became pregnant. In April 1944, I was born in Wenatchee. Later that summer, my parents moved to a new, larger home suitable to accommodate all four of us.

June Courtney Barnhart and husband Kenny Barnhart at the Courtney homestead. ca. 1942

June at the Courtney sawmill on the homestead. ca. 1942

As Mary and I got older, June started working outside the home. One of her first jobs was at the Valley Evaporating Company, feeding apples into a peeling and slicing machine where they were fed onto a conveyor belt and taken to the drying rooms. In the days before hi-tech, automated equipment, my mother, along with several dozen other women, stood on wooden platforms covered with pieces of carpet, shoving apples into the machines all day long. The large, steel building housing the equipment operated only in the winter, and because of inadequate heating, the women had to wear layers of clothing on the colder days. But June was not one to complain. She knew what hard work in adverse conditions was all about, and because she liked to be around other people, she enjoyed getting to know some of the other women. Coffee breaks in the heated lunchroom were welcome respites from the cold tedium at the machines, and the women were occasionally pretty lively. My sister, Mary and I sometimes visited Mom on her lunch break. Coming in from the cold, outside air to the loud laughter and the smell of sack lunches, coffee and dried apples inside, is a memory that stands out in my mind today.

My mother eventually shifted from work in the fruit industry to working as a waitress in restaurants and drive-ins, thoroughly enjoying the interaction with her co-workers and customers. For years she worked at F.W. Woolworth Company at the soda fountain. When the store closed in the mid-1960s, she received an award for outstanding service.

Before long, June started working at the Bus Depot Café, where she stayed until retiring in 1982.

June Courtney Barnhart next to a full load of freshly sawn timbers for the Holden Mine. ca.1943

In 1961, Mom acquired her first horse since leaving Stehekin, a mare named Beauty. She belonged to Ray, but was found to be slightly lame and couldn't endure the hard work required of a packhorse. He knew selling her would most surely mean she would end up as dog food, so we worked a deal to give her to Mom. Light riding and pulling a silky could be just fine. Living in town without a place to keep a horse, Mom rented a piece of land with a small barn on it in the foothills of West Wenatchee, where dad helped her put up a fence and get the water going. My father was never much of an animal lover and not very supportive of her horse endeavors, but that didn't slow her down. A small but determined woman, June made things happen. "Can't" was a word seldom, if ever, used by Mom. I remember going with her to feed a couple mornings one winter when the thermometer was hovering around five degrees. The six-volt battery in her old Plymouth barely turned over the engine, and she had to use starting fluid to get it started. No worries there. She raised the hood, sprayed a generous amount of the ether into the air intake, jumped into the seat and fired it up. I was impressed. I had never thought of my mother as one to know much about cars but, since the car was essential to taking care of the horse, she learned the basics. Mom always took an apple or a few carrots out to her horse. She called them treats; she got a kick out of watching Beauty eat. While she brushed and talked to the horse, I broke off a good size piece of hay from the bale for Beauty to eat, then, after thawing out a section of frozen pipe, filled the water tub. Before we left, June gave her another treat, a nice handful of oats, again spoke loving words while, lips quivering, Beauty vacuumed the oats from her hand. Those twice daily trips out to see her horse were the highlight of the day, even in adverse weather conditions. Just like her mother Mamie, June truly loved animals.

Finding that Beauty was not as sure footed as she hoped, in July 1962 June bought an eight-year old bay mare she named Queenie. Mom would never be without at least one horse, most always two, for the rest of her life. They were in her blood for good now. Her whole life revolved around the horses. They gave her a true sense of purpose. If she had to live in town, she could at least have a part of her heritage with her.

Later in 1962, Mom gave Beauty to the Washington State University School of Veterinary Medicine, where she would be used in studying lame horses and the cause and effects of their disabilities. The rest of Beauty's years were mostly spent out to pasture with other horses in the program—a pretty good life for a horse once destined for the cannery.

In 1965, Mom bought a two-year old buckskin gelding she named Gold Digger (Digger for short). Not being saddle broke, she hired a man to work with him for a few days until she could start riding him. While in training, Digger liked to buck a lot, which I think is pretty normal, but Mom thought a couple of times of renaming the horse Buck (I'm not sure if that was for *"buckskin"* or because he liked to buck). She actually referred to him as Buck in a couple journal entries, but stuck with the name Digger. In January 1966 Digger bucked June off for the first of several times. Reading through her journals is like reading about a rodeo event:

"April 5 1966: Rode today. Bucked off twice. I finally won though. July 25 1966: Bucked some today while cantering. I stayed on though. October 27 1966: Cantering and something happened. I fell off (or bucked off). Knocked me out. In the hospital four days. Rode him home though, he wasn't mean. April 26 1967: Bucked and reared

when I got on him today. I got back on and rode him after though. Didn't hurt me much. June 19 1968: Bucked me off while cantering tonight, just playing!"

Because of her size—barely five- foot-four and a hundred pounds—she looked more like a jockey sitting on top of those large horses. If they made up their minds to sidestep on the trail, or start bucking, it was hard for her to stay aboard. She never broke any bones, but a couple of times had the wind knocked out of her or was knocked out cold for a short time.

Shortly after buying Digger, June, needing more space and some pasture, found an acre of land for lease near her present location. The price was right, and she and dad went to work building a prefab barn and tack room—something that could be moved later if another, better, deal came up. Mom's records indicate she paid for every nail, screw and piece of plywood in the structure—even some tools. I think since Dad was giving her a hard time about the horses, out of stubbornness, she would pay for everything associated with them. Mom was that way—a very sweet and gentle person, but she could play hardball if the situation called for it.

June sold Queenie in October 1966 after having several incidents with her on the trails. She'd be going along fine, then something would spook her and she'd rear up, getting out of control. One time Mom was riding with another lady way up on Horse lake Road near the top, when they got off to have lunch. Queenie had one of her fits and the next thing they knew, both horses were heading hell-bent down the road. Mom and her friend had to walk several miles before they found her friend's horse, but not Queenie. After hunting all over in vain, they finally doubled up and rode on down to their cars. June, of course was furious! She worried about the saddle rolling and getting the horse tangled in the brush. Early the next morning, she drove back up to where they found the other horse and sure enough, there was Queenie, eating grass as if nothing had happened. Thanks to the breast collar, the saddle stayed on. She found the saddle blanket and bridle a short distance away. I think that was the proverbial straw that broke the camel's back. Mom had had enough of Queenie.

In February 1971, my parents bought ten acres of land at the mouth of Number One Canyon on the west side of Wenatchee. They moved the horse and barn to that location as soon as possible. Still working at their regular jobs, Mom and Dad were only able to work weekends at the new property, but they managed to plant and fence a large pasture area and put in about seventy five soft fruit trees, as well as the irrigation system. June kept riding almost daily after work. She worked the early shift at the Bus Depot Café, getting off work at eleven in the morning, allowing time to ride and work at the pasture in the afternoons. In 1972 she bought Meiko, a five-year-old buckskin mare to replace Queenie. Like old cars in Stehekin, you need more than one to be sure you have at least one that works.

In the early 1970s, Mom joined some of the horse clubs in the Wenatchee area, a good way to meet other horse people and to start going on overnight trail rides to the high country. The Back Country Horsemen of Washington appears to be with whom she rode the longest. June made many good friends and riding partners in the club. Overnight trips took them as far away as the Pasayten Wilderness Area to the north, Buck Creek Pass in the Glacier Peak Wilderness Area to the west, and The Clockum over to Ellensburg to the south. Her meticulous record keeping and journals contain entries about every ride she ever went on including the number of

June Courtney's first diary.

miles and any unfortunate incidents that took place on the trip—and there seemed to be a few. Had I known at the time of some of those "blow-ups" with the horses, I'm sure I would have worried a lot more about her out on the trail. I think I got spoiled during my time working for Ray with our old mountain horses. None of them were fancy, but for the most part, they knew how to behave on mountain trails. Working almost daily, the animals became conditioned and in tune with the mountains, where as with "town horses," they just never had that kind of daily exposure. Most people were looking for a horse that would look good in parades as well as in the mountains—a rare combination. I don't think any of our horses would have qualified for a parade. In one ten-year period, Mom logged 5,698 miles on three different horses.

When my father retired in 1974, he and June moved into a new home they were building on the foothills property. Now Mom could be with her animals day and night without driving the three miles, two or three times a day. She was thrilled to be there, living so close to the riding trails right from their back yard. Some days, she would saddle up one horse, take it out for a couple hours, then come back and do the same with the other one. Both horses had little quirks about them that needed work—Meiko not wanting to go in or out of the trailer and spooking on the trail, while Digger still liked to buck once in awhile. From time to time June would hire a man to help with the training, but cost kept that to a minimum. After one trail ride that went pretty well, it took four men to help her load Meiko back in the trailer. Needless to say, Mom was pretty disgusted about the whole thing. After reading about some of those fiascos, I was surprised how she put up with it so long. She kept Meico for almost twelve years before selling her to a friend who seemed to have better luck training her than Mom.

In October 1982, June retired from restaurant work. At sixty-four years old she was ready to spend more time with her horse out on the trails, but without a companion for Digger, she started looking again for another horse. In November 1983, she bought a four-year old quarter horse bay gelding called Ricky. A gentle horse, he got along well with Digger and it seemed that Mom finally had found a good trail horse. For the year 1984, she recorded almost seven hundred miles on Ricky, while only one hundred on Digger. Clearly, Ricky was her favorite horse, but she couldn't stand to sell Digger, so kept him around for short day rides above Wenatchee, and as company for Ricky.

Always impressed with my mother's obsession for work and house cleaning, I didn't realize how much that carried over to the horses until reading a journal entry at the end of a trail ride up the Icicle River:

"Friday, July 12 1985 – Clear and hot.
We broke camp, loaded up and left about 9 am. Stopped at Leavenworth for coffee, home about 10. Cleaned up, rested, did laundry and dusting. Also cleaned the pick-up and started to clean the tack. After dinner, I walked two miles down to Western Ave. and back."

"Saturday, July 13 1985 – clear and hot.
Did vacuuming and laundry, etc. Cleaned my leather tack, rested, went to Grange to get new spurs. Rode Ricky tonight, also washed halters and saddle pad. Washed the horse's feet. Walked to Western and back."

It goes without saying, Mom liked to stay busy. She wasn't one to sit around, waiting to get old, despite increasing problems with rheumatoid arthritis, mostly in her hands. At times you could tell she was in a lot of pain, but she always shrugged it off and kept busy. Exercise was her method of dealing with pain, and it seemed to work pretty well. As part of her daily routine, she did a regimen of push-ups, pull-ups and sit-ups, as well as other stretching exercises and, of course, riding and walking. For such a small woman, she was tough as nails.

Ever since Mom left Stehekin, she always made a special effort to come back for visits. In the early fifties, she and Dad started a cabin on a small piece of land just upriver from the old homestead cabin. Over the years, they added on and made improvements until they had a fairly comfortable place to stay, adding electricity and running water in 1964 after Chelan County PUD built the Stehekin Hydro Plant. Shortly after arrival, June always walked up to the hump, a favorite place she used to go as a child. Often, Nancy or I would go along and sit with her while she talked about her childhood. As a youngster, Mom spent a lot of time on the hump, writing in her journal or just enjoying the time alone. She spoke of sometimes taking the two horses, Brownie and Sally, up to graze in that lush grass. It was a special place, only a hundred feet or so above the valley floor and a half mile away. The large meadow-like area, with its stately pines and deep pine grass, gave one the impression of being far out in the wilderness, miles away from anywhere. My sister, Mary, and I, as well as our children and some of their children, have all followed that same path to Mom's special place.

June Courtney on the "hump" near the Courtney homestead. ca.1933

June Courtney Barnhart on Summit Trail pack trip with Cragg Courtney and other nephews.

Over the years, June continued to log impressive mileage on the trail rides. She took awards for various accomplishments such as most miles ridden, or most inspirational member, but by 1986, Digger was beginning to show signs of old age along with health issues. Mom had to quit riding him, but wanted to keep him as company for Ricky. She liked Digger a lot, but it soon became apparent that he was suffering too much. Finally, in 1990, she made the decision to have him put down. She made the following note in her record book of the event:

"Don Beardon came today to put Digger down. He has been sick for over a month. Had a bad cold, couldn't hardly walk. Just was feeling terrible. I cried for two days. It was so hard to part with him. He was my dear friend. We buried him in the pasture behind the barn."

Mom and Ricky spent a few more good years riding the trails, but arthritis began to slow my mother down, making it increasingly difficult to get in and out of the saddle. Another accident in 1998, when June turned eighty, seemed to be the turning point where she gave up riding for good. Ricky accidentally knocked her down with his head as she was reaching in his manger, severely spraining her right arm. Always making light of a bad situation, Mom said, *"But he didn't mean to."* After the cast came off and her arm was healing, June resumed her daily walks up to the end of the road, but it was not easy. Sore feet and the cold wind kept her home some days, though most always she was able to do the horse chores.

In addition to her physical disabilities, Mom was starting to show signs of dementia. The typical first signs of dishes and laundry put away in strange places gave way to more serious things such as forgetting to take her medicine or not remembering if she fed the

June Courtney Barnhart with daughter Mary standing in the corner of the old homestead cabin where she was born in 1918. ca. 1996

horse. She often spoke of wanting to come to Stehekin. June's mind was starting to shift back to her childhood, as if she were living in that era instead of the present. On April 12, 2000, over their sixtieth wedding anniversary, we managed to get my parents up here for the occasion. It was great to see them here taking short walks around the homestead in June's favorite time of year. It turned out to be her last trip to her family home.

The next two years saw declining health issues taking Mom away from us a little at a time. In 2002 she lost her balance in their living room, falling and cutting a deep gash in her leg on a Formica table. Dad took her to the emergency room where the doctor fixed her up and sent them home with explicit instructions on the importance of changing the dressings, cleaning the wound and taking antibiotics. They'd already found out from previous wounds that Mom's immune system was slowing down, and infections were a constant threat with open wounds that wouldn't heal. Between Dad's poor eyesight and Mom's lack of concern about the seriousness of the cut, they weren't able to give her the care needed. The doctor scheduled several appointments for cleaning and redressing, but my parents had to do their part as well, and it wasn't happening. The difficult decision was made to admit her to a nursing facility where June could get proper care.

Visits to see Mom were heartbreaking and emotionally draining. Most always, she'd be in the hallway, bent over in her wheelchair, picking at some imaginary piece of lint on the floor. Rarely did she even acknowledge our arrival. After a few minutes, she'd look up and mumble something unintelligible. We learned that talking about her childhood in Stehekin seemed to perk her up a little.

Fortunately, Mom didn't have to stay in the nursing home long. Late in the morning of November 22, after receiving a call from the nursing home that Mom was nearing her time, we drove over to be with her. Dad was already there, spending almost all of his time at the facility. Mom was resting peacefully, unaware of our presence. After spending most of the day there, Nancy and I stepped out to get a bite to eat. No sooner had we finished than we got another call from the nurse that we should hurry back. When we arrived, Mom's breathing was very slow and labored. Her eyes were closed. Briefly, her eyes opened, she took one last, large breath, and that was it. At last she was free of the pain and suffering. Of course, it was a terribly sad moment, but on the other hand, we were so relieved it was finally over. Mom had had a great, long life and she didn't need to suffer any longer. June was the last surviving member from her generation of the original Courtney family.

June Courtney Barnhart in the mountains she loved.

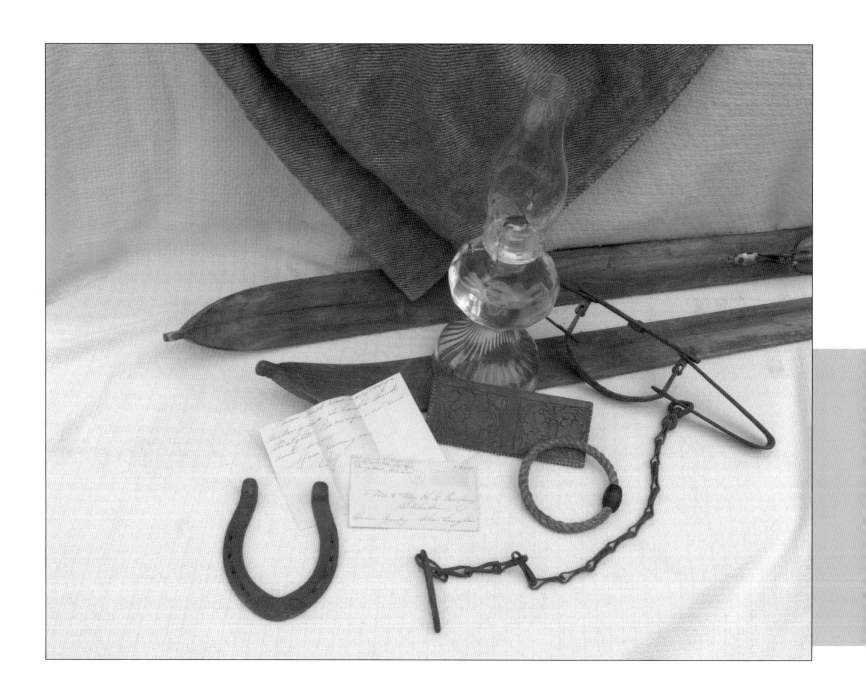

Part II – Chapter IV

James Ray Courtney
1920 – 1982

In 1955 at the age of eleven, I visited Ray and Esther for a week or so when they were living on the Company Creek Road at what is now Al Winkel's cabin. Virgil Fellows, Esther's brother, was staying with them while he and Ray were building the sawmill up on Ray's thirteen acres at the homestead. Virgil and I slept at a little camp at the mill and drove down to the house in the old boom truck for breakfast. I remember small poles on the ground around each sleeping bag site, making it feel more like a bed than sleeping on the ground. I was captivated by the whole experience of being out there, driving to breakfast in the dark in that old Army truck, and listening to a couple of World War II veterans swapping jokes and stories.

Mike and Dan at Washington Pass, 1962. Before the North Cascades Highway was built.

In 1958 I started working summers for Ray as a packer's helper, spending the next seven seasons mostly in the mountains above Stehekin. We made many memorable trips, packing anywhere from small family groups, to large Sierra Club outings numbering over a hundred people, sometimes teaming up with another packer or two in order to provide enough horses to carry the large amount of gear. As I reflect back over those seven summers, one trip into the Pasayton Wilderness Area comes to mind.

We had just finished a ten-day trip with thirty-five Sierra Club members and were deadheading the horses on a three-day ride back to Stehekin, fifteen miles of which were on gravel road down to Early Winters Creek. The details of the trip itself have faded, but the stop along the road at Bob Hadway's Lost River Resort was the highlight of the adventure. It was close to noon and we figured a good hamburger with all the trimmings would go well about then. We tied the horses to trees out in front of the small café and went in to look at the menu. While sitting at the counter talking to the owner, we discovered he was a pilot and his plane, an old fabric-covered Stinson, was parked out back ready to go. The next thing we knew, a deal was struck, and we were taxiing down the grass runway for a scenic flight over the area we had just left. Seeing those rugged and beautiful mountains from the air was certainly the icing on the cake. The pencil-line trails over sharp, jagged ridges looked impossible to navigate a pack string on; the lush meadows looked like putting greens in a deep forest. The flight lasted an hour, covering not only the Pasayten area, but also all the way over to the headwaters of the Stehekin Valley, close to Ray's ranch. Ray was tempted to have him land at the small Stehekin airstrip so he could go see his wife and children, but I knew if we did, he wouldn't want to go back, and I would be stuck bringing the horses home alone, a job I certainly wasn't too keen on. By the time we got back and on our way again it was about 4:00 pm., and another four or five hours of riding to get to Jack Wilson's Early Winters Resort, our stopping place for the night. We saw great country on the ground and from the air, a perfect way to end the trip.

Ray was born on May 10, 1920 in Winesap, Washington, a small group of farms located on the Columbia River halfway between Chelan and Entiat. The Courtney family lived in Stehekin, but Mamie, my grandmother, wanted to be closer to a doctor for Ray's delivery. Two years earlier, she had given birth to my mother,

June, in Stehekin, and although the delivery was okay, there were complications. My grandfather, Hugh, found a job on a ranch in Winesap, so in November of 1919 the family, along with the cows and other animals, packed up and moved downlake. When school got out in June, they moved back up to the homestead in Stehekin. Ray was the fourth and last child born to Hugh and Mamie.

Young Ray standing by the homestead cabin.

Thirteen-year-old Ray at the homestead.

Early on, Ray quickly learned about living in the woods. Different from the other boys, he liked to read, mostly books and magazines about survival, building emergency shelters, making skis and living in the wilderness. When he turned thirteen, he joined "The Open Road Pioneers Club," a national organization similar to the Boy Scouts of America. Promotions through the ranks were achieved by accomplishing different levels of woodsmanship, the highest being The Inner Circle. It didn't take long for Ray to reach that goal. A letter from Ray published in the magazine, The Open Road for Boys, April 1934 issue, after he received his Inner Circle pin, reads as follows:

Dear Deep River Jim,

We always have to make an eight-mile trip to get the mail in the winter. In summer, we sometimes use the Ford and go clear to the Post Office. You see in winter we hire a fellow to bring our mail as far as his place. He has a sleigh and team. The whole valley furnishes his hay so he will bring our mail as far as his place, and we have an eight mile trip to there and back. In summer we have to hike fourteen miles for the mail when we don't use the old Ford. So between helping get the mail and trapping, I am quite busy in the winter. I usually get letters from Pioneers when I make the trip and it well repays me for the tiresome journey.

Today, I made myself a new pair of skis from maple and I have them all ready for a good ski trip tomorrow. The maple was well seasoned and they are now ready for use.

My dad is a great camper and hunter and he is a dead shot with his 30-40 Winchester. I have never seen him miss his target with his faithful ole rifle, which is about thirty years old and has had such good care that it is almost as good as new. He knows pretty near all there is to know about these mountains and he is never tricked by snowslides, for he knows just when they will slide. He has camped, fished, hunted and roamed these mountains for years.

From our cabin we can see many avalanches, when it is wet weather, that come clear from the summits and go clear to the foot of the mountains, and they are many hundred feet deep. Our cabin is situated in a place that is safe from snowslides.

My father taught me how to make snowshoes and many other tricks of woodcraft. And the more one lives in the woods and wilderness the more he learns from experience.

We have our own cows and we always have plenty of milk, cream and good ole' homemade butter. We also have enough chickens so we have a good supply of eggs. In summer we raise a large enough garden so that when mother cans it up we have plenty of vegetables all winter. In summer, we practically live on our vegetables. All we must buy is flour, sugar and things such as this. So you see, we are all more or less Pioneers. And I want to tell you Jim, I never enjoyed anything more in my life than being a Pioneer.

Boy, I treasure my Inner Circle pin as I would a chest of gold. In fact, it means much more to me than money ever could.

J. Ray Courtney, Stehekin, Wash.

The cabin Ray built at the homestead when he was sixteen years old. (As seen at the Stehekin Valley Ranch)

Taking into account the imagination and part-time exaggeration of a fourteen-year old boy, the letter exemplifies how proud Ray was of the club and his achievement pin. It meant a great deal to him and set the course and principles from which he followed the rest of his life. When I was about fourteen, Ray gave me Deep River Jim's Wilderness Trail book—a well-worn, dog-eared copy printed in 1935, full of survival and how-to stories about living in the wilderness. As I thumb through the book today, I find several articles and illustrations of skills I saw Ray using when I worked for him in the late 1950s and early 1960s.

In the spring of 1935, at age fifteen, Ray started building a log cabin out in the woods behind the barnyard. Like the other boys, he wanted his own space. The previous year, he built a good trail out to the site and cleared the land. The trail was essential for getting the logs out to the building site. Several of the trees were cut nearby but wanting to maintain that deep-woods atmosphere around the cabin, he cut many of the others farther away, requiring more trails for skidding the logs out of the woods to the main trail. Whenever possible he used one of the horses for that chore but other, smaller logs were drug by hand. The 12x20 foot cabin, surrounded by large fir trees, had a warm and cozy feel to it. The cedar, split-shake roof extended over an eight-foot porch providing an excellent place for a good supply of firewood, further enhancing the setting of a cabin in the woods. I can picture Ray, as a youngster, sitting by the stove in his cabin, reading Deep River Jim's Wilderness Trail Book, by the light of a kerosene lamp.

Over the next several years, Ray continued to sharpen his skills as a woodsman and educated young man. He read voraciously anything he could get his hands on, from the dictionary to philosophy to drawing and penmanship. He also spent a lot of time helping find the horses and cows. The whole family took part in that chore, but once Curt and Laurence started working and living away from home, Ray and my mother, June, usually ended up with the honor. Often the hunt was combined with a trip to the landing or down the road to visit their half-sister, Dorothy Byrd, or friends. The animals had favorite places they liked to graze— the horses up on Company Creek bench or the hump, a grass covered bench just up-valley from the homestead, the cows down on the valley floor closer to water, most likely somewhere out on the island between the Lesh place and the river. Seeing fresh tracks heading off one way or another, Ray and June had clues about where to look on the way home. They got pretty good at second-guessing the animals.

Helping out with improvements and the daily chores around the farm also kept Ray busy. At one time, Mamie had three gardens on the property, requiring many hours of hard, manual labor, from the time the ground was tilled in the spring until the produce was harvested, canned and put away for winter. As with Curt and Laurence, logging and sawmill work was part of living on the Courtney homestead. With the help of Hugh, he learned to splice cable chokers, used for dragging logs to the mill. Those simple eye splices were the beginning of a secondary career splicing large and very long ski lift cables, keeping him employed in the off season when packing slowed down.

Another of Ray's achievements as a young man, was the art of rope spinning— twirling a loop of rope around very fast, and jumping in and out of the loop with fancy footwork similar to jumping rope, but you are the spinner and the jumper. Ray mastered the technique well enough to perform at a couple of rodeos while stationed in Colorado in the Army during the war. Entertaining his friends in the barracks helped pass the time on weekends as well.

Ray spinning a rope in front of barracks at Camp Roberts, California

Ray in his army uniform at Camp Roberts, CA. during basic training.

In June of 1942, barely twenty-two years old, Ray was drafted into the army. Curt had been drafted in December 1941, landing an assignment with the ski mountain troops at Fort Lewis, Washington. With the help of Curt pulling some strings and Ray's mountain skills, he was hoping for the same assignment. A letter dated June 30, 1942 written to Hugh and Mamie, spoke about basic training at Camp Roberts, California:

"Dearest Mom and Dad,
How are you all by now? I am pretty fine. It is really hot here but I don't mind too much. We have been drilling for two days now. They really pour it to us. But that is much better than sitting around. I am learning a lot of things. Nothing that I wouldn't gladly exchange for any of the times I have spent at home. How are you feeling Mom? And you too Dad? By golly you want to be taking care of yourselves. That is the only way to keep happy and keep us boys happy too. Remember that will you. I will be glad when I can get a letter from you. They told us today that we would not be here the full 13 weeks. I probably shouldn't be telling you this but I hope I am right in assuming that I will get into the mountain regiment sooner. Back to somewhere I can see you folks at least once in awhile. Of course there are things to consider. Somehow, I am still confident that everything is going to come out alright. I haven't got any mail yet but I know how it is. Notice that my address is 1st platoon now. It is pretty easy for the mail to get mixed so don't worry about slight delays. Tell me everything when you write, about the garden, mill, flowers, and just everything. Guess I will stop for now. It's pretty late. Be careful now and don't worry.

With love to the best mom and dad in the world,
Ray

P. S. Say Laurence, I sure would stress Dad's dependence on you in the mill in every way possible and defense work too. Better be working on it all the time. You sure won't be sorry if you don't get in here. Your loving brother,
Ray"

The above note to Laurence spoke of ways to keep from getting drafted, notably, helping Hugh earn a living in the mill, which, in turn was supplying timbers to Holden Mine, a defense contractor.

After basic training, Ray was, indeed, sent to Fort Lewis to the 87th Mountain Infantry Regiment, the same outfit Curt was in. They were in different companies but got to see each other most every night. Curt was working with mules and had access to the saddle shop where, on weekends and evenings, he and Ray made a variety of leather goods for guys in the outfit. Unlike other soldiers out on a weekend pass, Ray and Curt spent most of their paychecks buying leather and tools, barely having enough money to get back to camp. In addition to the small leather items such as wallets and belts, Ray became interested in building saddles. Whenever he could get time off, one of the men down in the leather shop, a saddle maker, helped him build his own saddle.

Ray and Curt stayed together for a little over a year, moving several times, even spending a few months in Kiska, Alaska. (See Chapter II, Curt). After returning from Kiska to Camp Carson, Ray was assigned to the 90th Light Infantry Division to continue mountain infantry training at Carson. While there, a job came up that he couldn't turn down. He was offered the duty of fireman, which sounds like what we think of as someone who puts fires out. At Camp Carson, in the winter, the job entailed shoveling coal into the furnaces for the barracks (ironically, a job I had while stationed there during the winter of 1966-1967). The beauty of that job is you work twelve hours on and twenty-four off, something that suited Ray just fine. He was exempt from all the marching, drilling and training the other troops had to endure, and the small group of firemen had their own quarters away from the large, sixty-man barracks. In a letter home, he asked Mamie to send his spinning ropes:

"...I'm still fireman and hope it stays that way. It is probably hard for you to understand why I do not try to get ahead but I would rather keep my friends and remain as I am. Say, would you send me my spinning ropes again? It seems I no sooner send them home than I want them again. I am not even sure where they are. Send all of them you can find will you and throw in a piece of fairly heavy rawhide will you? I would like enough to make hondas for the ropes."

Ray swimming at Guadalcanal.

(A honda is a piece of rawhide lining a smooth knot forming an eye at the end of a rope used particularly for lariats and spinning rope. The rawhide is soaked and formed around the inner part of the eye to keep the rope from wearing out).

"Be careful now and don't worry."

Your loving son, Ray."

In April 1944, Ray received orders to the replacement depot at Fort Ord, California, in preparation for loading on a ship bound for the South Pacific. Again, the spinning ropes had to be sent home. It was over a month before anyone heard from him, and now his letters were censored, not allowing him to say anything about where he was stationed. Later, after Japan surrendered in September 1945, and censorship was lifted, he explained in a letter to my mother the different islands where he served. The islands had already been secured from the Japanese, mostly about the time of the Battle of Coral Sea in 1942 and 1943. By the time Ray got there, the Allies were well established, providing support and refueling stops for planes heading farther west and eventually to Japan.

His first brief stop overseas was new Caledonia, then on to Guadalcanal. By the middle of June, he found himself on Bougainville in the 132nd Infantry but detached to work for the Combat Engineers in a sawmill. While on Bougainville, he wrote about meeting a fellow from Chelan named Virgil Fellows, saying he was a "good guy" and they "spent a lot of time swimming and hanging out together." A few years after the war, Ray became Virgil's brother-in-law when he married his sister, Esther.

Ray with native hunting spear, bow and arrow in the Philippine jungle.

After working in the sawmill for a while, Ray was permanently transferred out of the infantry to the 57th Combat Engineers, continuing to keep his job in the sawmill, working with guys, mostly from the Northwest, who had similar interests. He also became more interested in the natives, learning some of their customs and skills in rope making, weaving, and bow and arrow making, all from materials found in the jungle.

By the summer of 1945, Ray was once again transferred and on the move, this time to the Americal Division for a short time on the island of Leyte, then on to Luzon where he worked in a military post office for awhile. In July, shortly after Luzon was declared cleared of all enemy combatants, he wound up getting a job in the 1613th Engineer Forestry Company, in the mountains of Southeast Luzon, falling trees and logging for the sawmill. For the first time since going overseas, he was able to breathe fresh, mountain air and bathe in a cold stream running right next to camp. After the war ended in September 1945, leaflets were dropped by airplanes throughout the mountains of Luzon, explaining to the few Japanese soldiers still holed up, that the war was over and it was safe to come out. Ray mentioned in a letter that he saw a few of these stragglers, but they weren't a problem, and for the most part, they were also relieved the war was over.

After the war, the huge task of sending soldiers home began. A point system was developed to determine who got to go first. The criteria were based on length of service, time overseas, time in actual combat and rank. By October 1945, Ray had the required eighty-five points to leave the Philippines for home. He spent about two weeks at the Luzon Replacement Depot before boarding the ship for home.

Cliff Hopson, Dwight Crowder, Ray Courtney and Virgil Fellows on the summit of Bonanza Mountain, (Note Virgil's slick soled boots.)

Trapping cabin up Company Creek built by Ray Courtney and Virgil Fellows in the late 1940's.

In 1946, after getting settled back in Stehekin, Ray and Virgil Fellows became re-acquainted and started up Alpine Packers, guiding horse trips into the backcountry of the North Cascades. Their brochure listed several package mountain trips tailored to fit the needs for a variety of interests, including hunting, fishing and photography. Rates advertised were as follows: Pack and saddle horses, $3.00 per day, the guide-packer, $10.00 per day (horse included). They also built a trapping cabin five miles up Company Creek, spending a few days in the winters supplementing their income with furs. The summers of 1950 and 1951 turned out to be good seasons, when they contracted with the USGS (United States Geological Service) doing fieldwork in the North Cascades. On one trip to Holden Lake, they were fortunate to go along on a climb of 9,511-foot Bonanza Peak, the highest point in Chelan County. These were good times for Ray and Virgil. They both liked working for the geologists and learned a lot about the mountains they lived in. I remember in later years hearing them speak fondly of those days and the men with whom they stayed in touch for the rest of their lives.

When Ray and Virgil first started up the packing business, they also both became interested in two sisters living in the Methow Valley, the next major watershed east of the Stehekin Valley. The girls, Rhoda and Arlene Thew, lived in the small town of Twisp, about twenty miles as the crow flies from Stehekin. Ray met Arlene on a horse-buying trip while staying at a motel where she was working in the office. Before long, Ray started making more trips to Twisp, not only to look for horses, but also to visit Arlene. That winter, on at least one occasion, Ray skied across 6,064-foot Twisp Pass, an arduous, twenty-mile trek over some of the roughest terrain in the Cascades, to visit Arlene in the next valley. It didn't take long for the courtship to turn into marriage. Virgil and Rhoda met while he and his brother, Don, were in Twisp on business. He started talking to a man working on his car and out from underneath came his daughter, Rhoda, to see what was going on. After seeing Virgil, she decided he was the man she was going to marry. But Virgil wasn't ready to settle down yet. It would be another nine years before they married.

Ray and Arlene moved into a small cabin Ray built on part of the old Frank Lesh homestead on what is now the Al Winkel place. The cabin still stands today, basically looking the same as it did back then, with a few improvements. Curt bought the property while still in the Army and was selling it to Ray. Virgil and Ray built a corral and small saddle shed just to the south of the house, keeping the horses there only when they had trips planned. The rest of the time, the horses ran loose, grazing around the valley and up on the Company Creek benches. A couple days before a scheduled trip, they'd go out, find the horses, and bring them home until the trip started. That was the way Hugh did it, and for the most part it worked pretty well, since feed was expensive and there was plenty of good grass growing in and around the valley. Until, that is, some of the local resort owners started complaining about the horses getting on their newly planted lawns or walking and rolling in their water systems at the head of the lake.

When discussions to create a herd district failed on the local level, a petition was presented to the County, asking that a herd district be formed to force the owners of the horses to keep them fenced. Not wanting to create another county agency and be the bad guys in the middle of a Stehekin dispute, the County arbitrated a meeting between the opposing parties, hoping a settlement could be reached. Finally, it was agreed by all concerned that the locals would all get together and build a cattle guard at Company Creek,

keeping the horses up on this side of the river and away from the resorts. The county would re-visit the issue in six months to see "how things work out." The cattle guard was never built and the conflict just seemed to go away, although I do remember a couple of other times when, not only Ray and Virgil's horses, but Guy Imus's as well, were discovered on the lawns. Guy was another packer in the valley and pretty good friends with the resort people, spending many an evening sipping cocktails on the patio at the landing. That seemed to smooth things out, and everything went back to normal.

During those early years when Ray and Virgil were booking mountain trips, the Forest Service decided to replace the old Agnes Gorge suspension bridge, two-and-a-half miles up Agnes Creek, with a new truss bridge near the confluence of the Stehekin River and Agnes Creek. It was disappointing to the locals to hear this news. The gorge was a scenic attraction in itself, but the walk over on the suspension bridge, or better yet, the horseback ride across, was an adventure, and the only way to get a good view of the gorge, some one hundred feet below. Since Ray wanted to keep using the gorge trail and bridge for the horse trips, he met with the Forest Service where an agreement was reached for him to buy the bridge for a dollar if he would put a locked gate on each end to keep the general public off the bridge and take full responsibility for any injuries his guests incurred. The deal worked fine for a while until some higher-ups in the Forest Service heard of it and decided the liability was too great to have such an agreement. Because Ray was the new owner of the bridge, he was forced to take it out. The Forest Service declared it unsafe for any travel…and it was on their land. That didn't set well with Ray, but his hands were tied and there was nothing he could do.

Agnes Gorge suspension bridge.

Laurence and Ray got together to come up with a plan to remove the bridge. They decided to take as much of the wooden structure off as they could, then cut the cables and let the rest fall into the gorge. They soon realized that hacksaws wouldn't make a dent in steel cable. The next time they took dynamite, blasting the cables off successfully, first one side, then walking the five miles around to shoot the other side. This little episode with the Forest Service didn't improve Ray's attitude about government agencies. He grew up listening to Hugh rant and rave about "educated fools" working for the Forest Service, and now began to understand what his dad was talking about.

On September 1, 1948, Ray and Arlene had their first child, a son named Bruce. Their second child, Sylvia was born on June 7, 1950. But 1950 turned out to be a tough year. Ray's mother, Mamie, was having serious health issues and after a short time in the Chelan Hospital, passed away on December 5. It was a huge blow to Hugh and all of the children. Once referred to as the "best mom in the world," Mamie was loved deeply by all. Her wisdom and good sense of humor kept the family just about as close-knit as any family could be.

About that same time, Ray and Arlene's marriage started to fail. The rough, backwoods lifestyle of Ray's was not an easy life. Raising two small kids in a small, remote cabin, without power or running water, in the woods of Stehekin, caused added stress to the marriage, already strained by the loss of my grandmother. It wasn't in the cards for Ray and Arlene to stay together, and by spring of 1951, they decided to get a divorce. Arlene and the children moved to Chelan while Ray continued to live in Stehekin and pursue his dreams.

Virgil's sister, Esther, started working for Beryl at the coffee shop in about 1948. She had been dating Ray's brother, Curt, part of the time, but when Beryl's husband Jack Blankenship passed away in 1948, Curt and Beryl started dating, getting married in 1950. Eventually, Ray and Esther got together and married in 1952. Ray had finally found his soulmate. He and Esther made a perfect match. She was a strong woman and didn't hold back when Ray's mountain ideas sometimes needed a little tweaking, letting him know how she wanted to be treated.

Their first son, Jim, was born in January 1953, followed by Tom in July, 1954. In November 1955, Gorden was born.

The Ray Courtney family. Ray, Esther holding Cragg, Jim, Gordy and Tom.

Jim, Gordy, Tom and Ray at the old Maxwell homestead cabin at what is now Stehekin Valley Ranch. Photo by Jim Trappe.

In 1955, after the Forest Service started offering small timber sales in the Stehekin Valley again, Ray and Virgil built a sawmill on the thirteen-acre piece of land Hugh and Mamie deeded to him from part of the homestead. The log deck and foundation of the old mill at Granddad's was rotting and in need of extensive repairs, prompting them to build a new mill closer to Battalion Creek where they could run a high pressure pump to clean logs. Because veterans had priority obtaining military surplus equipment, they bought a heavy duty two-and-a-half ton, four-wheel drive truck with a winch on the front, to which they added a large A-frame boom for lifting logs and other heavy loads—a valuable piece of equipment to have in the valley in those days. They also purchased a Guiberson, nine-cylinder radial diesel engine, formerly used in a military tank, for powering the sawmill. Radial engines have a distinct sound all their own, and the Guiberson could be heard all over the valley on a calm day.

Earning a year-round living in Stehekin from a sawmill and a pack string was next to impossible. In 1958, Virgil and Rhoda moved to Nepal where he took a five-year job with Riblet Tramway as superintendent on a long, aerial tram connecting remote villages to larger towns. Ray continued packing and running the mill in the summer months, trapping in the winter and working at ski areas. In 1958, he and Esther purchased twenty acres of the old Maxwell homestead, including the run-down house and the large field across the road. On May 6 of that year, their fourth son, Cragg, was born. That summer, part of my work, along with the other two young fellows Ray hired, was building fence around the field and helping clean up the old cabin to make it livable. We tore off the kitchen part and filled in the rat-infested well underneath it. The plan was to use only the two-story log structure, which was salvageable. Between pack trips, we continued to work at the ranch

Ray Courtney, Guy Imus, Bogue Morgan and Billy Sullivan at Washington Pass. ca. 1963. Photo by Mike Barnhart.

while living at Lloyd and Amy Bell's house near the mouth of the Stehekin River. That winter, Ray and the family moved to White Pass Ski Area, where he took a job running the poma lift to earn money to pay off the recent land purchase. In the spring of 1959, the family moved back to the ranch in Stehekin. They lived in a large Army pyramid tent in the maple grove on the far side of the field until work was completed on the Maxwell house. They moved into the house later that summer. That winter, on December 17, son Mark was born.

The packing business grew, and by 1960, we were kept busy all summer and into hunting season. One trip, that became an annual event around July 4th, was taking a small group of librarians and Wenatchee World folks to Heaton Camp on McGregor Mountain. One of the little side trips we did was over on the ridge to our south overlooking the Stehekin Valley. We started calling this ridge "Old Librarians' Ridge" in honor of the two librarians, Jo Pardee and Bo Brooks, who so loved the annual trek. There was always lots of fun bantering going on and the word "old" was just something that came out, even though the gals certainly weren't old. The name stuck, and the ridge has been called that ever since. Somewhere along the line, the word "old" was dropped by most, but a few of us still call it by the original name.

Before the North Cascades Highway was built, Ray contracted with the Sierra Club to provide all the stock and wranglers for a ten-day trip to Washington Pass. As I recall, there were just over one hundred hikers on the trip, plus thirty-four head of horses and mules. There were six of us wranglers, including Guy Imus, the other packer in the valley, his two helpers, and myself and another fellow working for Ray.

Making up horse loads of the mountain of gear was an enormous undertaking. The kitchen outfit itself included propane stoves (and tanks); large, round twenty-inch military surplus cooking pots; square washtubs, with the bottoms cut out and toilet seats attached for the latrines; piles of cook tents and tarps; along with what seemed like a pick-up load of miscellaneous rope, gas lines, axes, shovels, and the list goes on. The stack of cases of gallon-size cans of food was staggering. Then, of course, there were over one hundred duffle bags for the hikers. At least half of the bags had a round plastic washbasin in the bottom, which seemed like a good

Going to Cloudy Pass up the switchbacks from head of Agnes Valley. Ray Courtney, Pete Marlow and the head of Dan, Mike Barnhart's riding horse.

place to put it, I guess, but for the packers, making a diamond hitch stay on that hard, round-bottomed duffle bag was not a good way to start out the day. Those bags had to be set aside so they could be wrapped in a canvas manny tarp, or used as top packs.

It was like packing an army. Some of the more awkward loads, like those big cooking pots, could only be loaded on certain horses – those that wouldn't spook when their load rubbed the rocks or trees on a narrow section of trail. One horse stood out from all the rest as being the most sure-footed, levelheaded animal. Her name was Nellie, a big, strawberry roan mare. Not the prettiest of the lot, and a bit hard to catch, but steady as a rock. I really think Nellie took pride in being chosen for the worst loads. Ray had little rhyming phrases for some of the horses and Nellie's was "Big fat Nellie with the buckskin belly."

Ray Courtney, Mike Barnhart and Esther Courtney at McAllister Lake, ca. 1964. Photo by Hugh Blonk - The Wenatchee World.

Pack string heading to camp just below Cloudy Pass. Ray Courtney in the lead. ca. 1961

Once camp was set up on the edge of the meadow just west of the pass, we had to make two or three re-supply trips back down Bridge Creek, where a U-haul van belonging to the Sierra Club was parked and used as a storage unit for the rest of the food. Fresh meat and produce was shipped up the lake on pre-arranged days and brought up to Bridge Creek by Curt or one of the guys working at the landing. Those overnight trips usually only required six or eight packhorses and two packers. Once, when I rode down with Guy Imus, we had the luxury of staying in the snow survey cabin with real beds, a stove, and a table to eat off of, something to look forward to when you spent most of the summer out in the hills sleeping on the ground.

Realizing those very large groups were not the most friendly to the environment, the Sierra Club and other hiking clubs started organizing smaller groups of about thirty-five people. The Sierra Club called theirs the "North Cascades Highlight" trips. Since one pack outfit could handle a group this size, life on the trail got a lot easier and less complicated.

On June 16, 1961, Esther gave birth to their last son, Clifford. Everyone was holding their breath in hopes for a girl, but that wouldn't happen for a few more years. That same year, Ray and Esther started organizing their own full service trips, including pack outfit, tents, kitchen and cooks. They called them the "Hike and Like it" trips. They even mailed a duffle bag to those who signed up so we didn't have to deal with all sizes and shapes of bags. That helped a great deal in streamlining the sorting and making up of pack loads. Other, smaller trips were booked throughout the summer as well, but the all-inclusive trips turned out to be quite popular, and we tried to do at least two a summer. Esther was involved in the planning and ordering of supplies. But with little

kids at home yet, she couldn't go along, so they hired Amy Bell as the cook. The first Hike and Like It trip was in the Glacier Peak Wilderness Area, where we camped several nights each at Buck Creek Pass and Cloudy Pass.

In the fall of 1962, when Chelan County PUD let the contract for building nine miles of distribution line in the Stehekin Valley, Ray signed on as a pole climber—another skill he learned while working in the logging camps of the Philippine Islands. A light snow year allowed him to work most of the winter. Although Ray appreciated the winter's work, he and Esther didn't want power to their house. The line ended about two miles downvalley from their place, where they were used to not having power and liked the simpler, less complicated lifestyle. Other than a very small DC Pelton-type wheel, mostly for lights that Tom put in for them, Ray and Esther lived out their lives without public power.

In August 1962, we packed sixty-five members of the Chicago Mountaineers into Pelton Basin, just below Cascade Pass. Esther cooked on that trip with the help of young Tom and Jim, as well as the rest of us. We used gas stoves and other kitchen equipment borrowed from the Sierra Club, since they stored a lot of their gear at the Courtneys' place anyway. Just prior to the people getting there, we made a trip in with the kitchen set-up to have the evening meal all ready on the day the group arrived.

Since a group of that size required about every horse we had, and wanting to avoid hiring other packers, strict weight guidelines were sent to the Mountaineers ahead of time. It was imperative they were followed. Though the trail was only five miles long, the group was coming in on the passenger boat, loading up, and bussing to Cottonwood Camp, then hiking to the basin. It was nearly three o'clock by the time they arrived along with their gear at Cottonwood Camp.

As we started laying out the horse loads, we discovered the club was thirteen hundred pounds overweight—ten or twelve horse loads worth! A second trip was unavoidable. On top of that, unbeknownst to us, one of the worst thunder and lightning storms of the decade was brewing up.

The rain started about the time we arrived in camp with the first load. By the time we unpacked the horses and helped set up a drying tent, it was getting late, and the storm was settling in for keeps. The trip back down was wet and dark. The ride from Basin Creek to Cottonwood was particularly lively as the thunder and light flashes bouncing around those huge rocks made it seem like a war zone. Wet and tired, we just wanted to get down, pack up, and get back, which we did, at about one-thirty in the morning.

The next day was a layover day, and we got to catch up on much needed sleep. However, since we were furnishing everything on the trip, there seemed to be no end to the work involved— firewood to drag out of the woods, tents to readjust, ditching around tents, carrying water from the creek, and helping Esther with kitchen chores. We even put up a tent sauna down by the creek that was a huge success, as the weather was cool and wet. Late August storms in the high country are a prelude to winter, and that storm was no exception.

The following day, I took a few horses back to Cottonwood Camp, planning to drive down to Sam Tolber's freezer to get another load of fresh meat and supplies. With a good early start from camp, I planned on getting back late that afternoon. But what started out as a pretty easy day turned into a nightmare. Little did I know about the road damage from the storm a couple days earlier.

No sooner had I started down the road in the Courtney Volkswagen Microbus than I came to a tree across the road. With an old handsaw and a rope, I managed to get the tree cut and out of the way. Well into the night and sixteen trees later, I got as far as Dolly Varden Camp where the road was washed out. There was nothing I could do but walk the rest of the way to Courtneys'— about four miles. By then, it was starting to get daylight. From there, I rode a bike on down to Sam Tolber's, where I borrowed a car, loaded up the supplies and started back up the road. After carrying the food across the washout and reloading everything into the microbus, I drove on to Cottonwood Camp. This time, I had a chainsaw to open up the road where I detoured through the brush the night before. Just as I came around the bend in the road at Cottonwood, I saw Ray, a serious look on his face, pulling into Cottonwood with a string of horses. Before I had a chance to explain, he started in, obviously thinking I had decided to stay the night. It wasn't a pretty sight. I tried to explain about the road, but by then his emotions had taken over, and he couldn't hear a word I said. About the time those pristine woods were echoing with our raised voices, Ray finally caught on to what I was trying to say. When it came to jumping to conclusions, with a splash of anger thrown in, our ancestors, notably his dad (my grandfather), had passed on a healthy dose of those genes to both of us, and that August 18, 1962 was probably the finest display of them either of us had ever shown toward each other.

Once things settled down and we could finally talk to each other, we got back to the business at hand— loading up the supplies and getting them up the trail to camp. By nightfall, all was forgiven, and

Camp near Cloudy Pass. ca. 1961

Loading Horses at Lucerne on Tom Courtney's landing craft, July 1982, after a trip from the upper Entiat valley to Lake Chelan. Pictured left to right: Mark, Jim, Ray, Cliff Courtney, and Scottie Bigelow

we had a good laugh over it. Every year when the 18th of August rolls around I think of that day; ironically, sixteen years later that turned out to be the wedding day of my wife, Nancy, and me. I continued working for Ray through 1964, at which time Uncle Sam was calling, and I went into the Army for three years. I wasn't all that concerned, really, as it was time to move on to new adventures.

Ray and Esther, with the help of sons Jim, Tom and another older wrangler, continued running the pack business. A couple of Esther's younger brothers also helped from time to time, but once again, Esther became pregnant with child number seven, keeping her out of the back country for a short time. At last, Esther's wishes came true when daughter, Peggy Ann, was born July 5, 1967.

As the debate heated up over the impending creation of the North Cascades National Park, Ray found himself, like many of us, caught between a rock and a hard spot. Rumors flourished about the threat of a road down Bridge Creek and widespread logging throughout the Stehekin watershed, influencing people's thoughts back and forth between park control and continued Forest Service management. If we went along with the Forest Service, would there really be a road and logging? Where were those rumors coming from? Were they planted out there by environmental groups wanting to see the Stehekin Valley included in the National Park? Those were questions Ray and everyone else in the valley wanted answers to. A letter he wrote to the *Wenatchee World* articulated his concerns:

"I have read with much interest recent articles and editorials about building a road to make the Stehekin Valley accessible. Has anyone bothered to ask residents of the valley what they think? This smacks of a Hitler "liberation."

By the same sort of reasoning, if toothpicks were in demand, for instance, after a chamber of commerce banquet, supporters of such roads would blithely smash a rare old Stradivarius and pass around the splinters. If the majority of the banquet didn't like violin music, or happened not to have the background to appreciate the exquisite masterpiece, the violin would only be a fiddle. Probably, it would not take too clever talking to convince most everyone that "longhairs" are a little odd anyway. Furthermore, if it were smashed quickly, old what's-his-name won't even notice.

The analogy fits. To those who do not take the trouble to listen to or study violins, the finest instrument in the hands of a master only produces fiddling. To those who never get out of their cars far enough or long enough to appreciate it, unspoiled country is just wasted space and should be used for something practical, like, say, toothpicks.

Whether you are a Democrat, Republican, or what have you, you will probably agree with the late President Kennedy's appraisal of our pitiful flabbiness. Does a nation as rich and great as ours have to surrender its last square miles to the car? More and more people of all ages are hoping to find a respite from modern tensions by getting away from the highway and all that it means, if only for a short time. Ask the people who come to Stehekin.

"Do it now," the road builders say. By all means—hurry—before thinking people can understand how their own money would be used to do irreparable damage to their own country.

The cross-state highway plan itself is a monument to the misappropriation of tax money and reeks of "axes to grind," but if we support a road connecting the Stehekin Valley to the highway we will deserve the inevitable. To fish shoulder to shoulder for minnows fresh from the hatchery; to park our cars side by side and hope to get a snap-shot of a harried, panting buck; and to gaze at the mural over the bar for unspoiled scenery as we drown our sorrows and remember the way it was."

Ray Courtney
Stehekin

The letter clearly expresses Ray's concerns. We have to remember, it was written in the 1960s, but it speaks to an uncertain future for the Stehekin Valley that is still going on today.

Ray and I attended a couple of House Interior Committee Hearings at the Benjamin Franklin Hotel in Seattle in April 1968. The hearing room was so overcrowded, an extra room had to be opened up. Congressman Morris Udall presided over one meeting and Congressman Roy Taylor the other. A lottery system was used to determine witnesses to be heard first after the testimony by government and leaders of private groups. If time ran out, written testimony would be received instead of oral testimony. Each person was allowed three minutes to speak. Ray was chosen, but time has faded my memory as to what he said.

The North Cascades National Park, Ross Lake National Recreation Area and Lake Chelan National Recreation Area were established later that year, with Stehekin included in the Recreation Area, not the Park proper. A new era was about to begin.

In 1969, the *Wenatchee World* contracted with the Courtney family to furnish the complete outfit, including food, cooks, wranglers and horses, for what was to become an annual event called the *Wenatchee World Trail Hike*. They sponsored the trips, putting ads in the paper, along with a sign-up form. Several employees of the newspaper, along with other folks, joined the excursions year after year into the high country of the North Cascades.

Tragedy struck the Courtney family in the summer of 1971 when fifteen-year-old Gordy drowned in an accident at the old millpond, one mile up the road from the landing. He and some other boys were playing on paddleboats in the pond when his boat tipped over, possibly hitting him in the head. By the time help arrived, he had been under water for about fifteen minutes and, despite resuscitation efforts on the floatplane to Chelan, he was pronounced dead at the Chelan Hospital.

Over the years, Ray, wanting to get a winter ski touring business going to augment their summer income, was formulating a plan to hire a certified ski instructor to teach and lead ski tours up the unplowed road to the Ranger Cabin at Bridge Creek. About 1973, his nephew, Robert Byrd, successfully won the bid for the restaurant and lodge concession at the landing, where he and Ray worked a plan to base the ski operation. They set up the ski room in the lobby of the Swissmont Lodge, and in December 1973, Nancy Apthorp, the new ski instructor from the Boston area, arrived as the only passenger on the boat that day. Package tours were booked at the lodge, providing room and board, rental skis with instruction and, for those having the ability, a trip in to the cabin, where, at the higher elevation, snow conditions were much better than down in the valley. Cross-country ski trails were established and marked around the valley, and shuttle busses made scheduled trips between the Courtney Ranch and the landing, allowing guests to get out and explore winter in Stehekin. The operation was a good idea, but several factors contributed to its demise, mainly transportation to Stehekin. The winter boat schedule made it impossible to come here for a weekend without

Ray splicing cable at Mission Ridge Ski Area. The splice will cover 125 feet when finished. Photo by Hugh Blonk, The Wenatchee World.

taking Friday and Monday off from work— something a lot of folks couldn't do. Warmer temperatures also played a role. People could drive to the Methow Valley for a weekend, get drier snow, groomed trails, and not miss any work; pretty hard to compete with that. By 1979, the ski touring business shut down for lack of interest.

The next couple of years, Ray kept busy with the summer pack trips and winter splicing jobs. He turned sixty in the spring of 1980, but kept fit as a fiddle and going strong. The whole family was involved in the trips now, along with a couple other women to help Esther with the cooking. Often, with a bigger crew now, they could run more than one trip at a time. In July 1982, I went on a trip with Esther, Mark, Jim and about twenty guests, from the upper Entiat Valley to Lucerne, about ten miles south of Stehekin on Lake Chelan. When the trip finished at Lucerne, Ray and his crew had just finished up a trip from the Glacier Peak Wilderness Area and met us at the lake. Tom was also there with his landing craft to take some of the horses and a few of us back to Stehekin, while Ray and his crew headed back up Railroad Creek with fresh supplies, the rest of the horses and his helpers for the return trip to Stehekin with another group. I shot several black and white photos of the horse loading operation, showing Ray and the others putting the horses on, alternately head to rear across the landing craft, a rather unusual sight that I wanted to record on film. Turns out, it was the last time I saw Ray and those were the last photos I took of him.

On August 10, 1982 Ray died while bringing a string of packhorses over Hilgard Pass in the Glacier Peak Wilderness Area. Some of the horses got tangled on a steep switchback, and as Ray was trying to straighten them out, he and three horses went over the side, rolling more than a thousand feet. He died instantly. Also on the trip were his wife, Esther, his son, Mark, and cook/wrangler Scottie Bigelow, along with twenty-nine Wenatchee World trail hikers, many of them longtime Courtney friends.

Mark hiked out to Holden to radio for help, while Esther stayed with Ray's body. Scottie, Wilfred Woods, (owner of the Wenatchee World), and others helped bring the rest of the horses, and what gear they had left, into camp. Most of the kitchen gear and many of the tents had been lost when the horses went over. Soon, the medivac helicopter came in with the other Courtney boys to help set up a makeshift camp, for one last night, while Esther and Mark rode out with Ray on the helicopter—the tragic end to a lifetime in the mountains of a man who died doing what he loved the most.

Ray Courtney

Photo by Tracy Warner,
The Wenatchee World

ALPINE PACKERS
"High Country Pack Trips"
STEHEKIN, WASHINGTON

PACK AND SADDLE HORSE AND GUIDE SERVICE

RAY COURTNEY   VIRGIL FELLOWS

Alpine Packers business card and brochure. ca. 1947

Guiberson military tank engine used to power Ray and Virgil's sawmill in Stehekin. ca. 1955

ALPINE PACKERS

High Country
Pack Trips

INTO THE AREA NORTH OF
LAKE CHELAN

RAY COURTNEY   VIRGIL FELLOWS

Stehekin, Washington

Alpine Packers

In the mountains north of Lake Chelan there is one of the last great wildernesses in America. There are little visited valleys, high passes with deep meadows, sparkling streams, and glaciated peaks, rugged and high, many of which are unclimbed. The streams are famous among fishermen, and deer, bear and mountain goats are seen often by those who go into the region. It is equally a vacation land for the fisherman, the hunter, the photographer and the person who just likes to be among scenes of great mountain beauty.

Our saddle and pack horses and pack services are available for trips into this high country from June through October.

A TRIP OF UNUSUAL SCENIC INTEREST is the Holden to Stehekin circle trip. The first camp is made on the shore of Lyman Lake, a tarn at the end of Lyman Glacier. There are many flowers in season and numerous peaks tower over the camp ground. The route then goes over the Cloudy Pass, one of the finest passes in the Cascades and down the Agness Valley and then out by way of Stehekin. The trip can be started from either end, and is one of the most beautiful trips to be had anywhere. Minimum time of this trip is four days.

FOR THE FISHERMAN an exceptionally fine trip is the Rainbow Valley to Bridge Creek trip. Excellent fishing is offered in Rainbow Creek and on over the pass at the head of Rainbow Creek in McAlester Lake. Going on down McAlester Creek, we reach Bridge Creek. By a short side trip, Rainy Lake and Lake Ann may be visited on this tour. These waters are all fine fishing. Four days are required to complete this trip from either direction, staying one night at each camp.

For those who wish to be packed to a camping place and left to be packed out at a later date set by them, there are many fine spots which can be reached in one or two days from the Stehekin Valley; Park Creek Pass area; Cascade Pass and Doubtful Lake area; Upper Bridge Creek, including Lake Ann and Rainy Lake; Suiattle and Cloudy Pass area and many others to choose from. On any of the pack trips we will furnish saddle horses, or you may walk if you desire.

We are equipped to furnish all the necessary camp supplies and equipment with the exception of sleeping bags, hunting or fishing tackle, and personal items. Or if you wish, you may bring your equipment supplies. If you are not well acquainted with this area, we will be glad to help you plan a trip to suit your requirements, and upon request, we will furnish sample equipment and food lists which have proven satisfactory.

FOR THE HUNTER we will be packing into virgin hunting country this fall. A region where many deer, bear, mountain goat and upland game birds abound. The hunting area is not crowded and is among the finest.

Rates vary according to the number of persons in the party, the amount of equipment furnished and the duration of the trip.

Pack and saddle horses—
$3.00 per day for one to six days.
$2.50 per day after six days.

The Guide-Packer—
$10.00 per day. (horse included).
$8.00 per day after three days

Special Rates—
For trips longer than one week.
Reductions for large parties.
Flat rates for hunters according to distance packed.

Reservations necessary for prompt, efficient service. When writing, it will save time to state the number of persons, approximate dates and the amount of time you want to spend on the trip.

ALPINE PACKERS,
Stehekin, Washington.

Part II – Chapter V

Harwood Lotspiech
1904 – 1968

I knew Harwood for the first twenty-four years of my life, but can't say that I really knew him that well. While growing up in Wenatchee, we only lived a few blocks away from his family, getting together occasionally for dinner on holidays. He also came by to visit Mom sometimes, but when I was small, his appearance and gruff personality frightened me just a little. Slightly disfigured from a mining accident, his mouth had a twist to it, which to a kid with any imagination, made him look mean, though he really wasn't. He liked to tease and roughhouse, but after I got older, I learned how to tease right back, and things were fine after that. Harwood was a big man, and like so many men from that era, he worked hard at physical labor most of his life. His nickname was Blackie, and most everyone called him that. He seemed to be a man down on his luck some of the time and didn't always come out on the winning end of business transactions. New acquaintances didn't quite know how to take him. I often wondered if the nickname came from the color of his hair, or from years working underground in the mines at Holden and Horseshoe Basin.

Born April 19, 1904 to Mamie and William Lotspiech at Moore point on Lake Chelan, Harwood spent most of his first six years at the Moore Hotel, owned by his grandparents, J. Robert and Mary Moore. His father, William came to work at the hotel in 1902 when Mamie was sixteen, and after a brief courtship, they married on November 3, 1903. After Harwood was born, Mamie and Billy, as she called him, moved to Wenatchee where they rented a house in town while William looked for work. As of early July, Harwood still didn't have a name. In response to a letter from her mother asking why, Mamie offered an explanation: "… No we have not given baby a name yet as we want to get one that won't be nicknamed, but I guess it will be pretty hard as they most always nickname them. I think I will name him Harwood, as I like the name. Thank Papa very much for the money he sent. It is so good of him. I am going to fix some more shirts for baby, as he is growing too big for those he has. He lays and admires his hands lots of the time now. I guess he thinks they are pretty. He has brown eyes and everybody says he looks just like me."

It is unclear if Mamie did in fact officially give the name Harwood to him at that time. She and her mother both referred to him as "baby" or "our little man" for the next several months. Below, Mamie talks about life in Wenatchee:

"June 24 1904
My Dearest Mother,
I have not got a letter from you since a week ago Monday. I hope you are all well up there. We are getting along very nicely and baby is getting cuter every day. He will lay on the bed and watch the coo coo clock now and be as happy as if I was holding him. Will you please have Molly (the horse) sent down to the eagle transfer Company as soon as you can. We think we can sell her as they want riding horses and they are quite scarce here. Have you any boarders yet? We got the papers alright and I see by the Leader (Chelan Newspaper) that Papa has another man working for him now. Mrs. Otis Darnell beat me three pounds on the baby question as her baby weighed 13 pounds when he was born. I don't think you could guess how much baby weighs now. I went down to the store Saturday and got him weighed and he weighs 14 pounds now. I think that's pretty good don't you? I just had a visitor, a Mrs. Mills who lives across the alley from us. How is the garden getting along and did your Morning Glories grow. I suppose that you have lots of roses by this time. I don't see many flowers here and it seems so funny not to as there are so many up

there. How are the cows and calves getting along now? Does Black give much milk? I am afraid she will get killed this winter as she was fresh so early in the summer. Well, I must close for now. I hope you will write soon.

With Love and kisses from your loving daughter,
Mamie Lotspiech.

In the early fall of that year ,Mamie got the flu and was terribly concerned Harwood would get it, so she sent for her mother to take the baby to Moore Point until she got better. Mrs. Moore was delighted to have her "little man" to pamper. She loved children,

Harwood and Dorothy with cougar on the dock at Moore Point.

and after Mamie moved to town, Mary became awfully lonely. For the next few weeks, Harwood stayed at the hotel with his grandparents while Mamie recuperated from her illness. In late October, Mary returned Harwood to Mamie and Billy.

A year later, in the fall of 1905, Mamie was expecting another child, while she and Billy were having disagreements over where to live. Billy wanted to return to Moore and work for Mamie's father, but she was against that idea, thinking it best they live away from the family, on their own. For the immediate future though, at the strong urging of Mary Moore, Mamie and Harwood did move back to the hotel, as Billy went off looking for work. After her second child (Dorothy was born in late December), Billy failed to stay in touch with Mamie so, not having much choice but to continue on at the hotel, she and the children settled in. One day, after over a year had passed without word from him, Billy wrote announcing that he'd changed his mind and wanted Mamie and the children to join him downlake. Taking advice from her mother and father, she decided to stay at the hotel with the children. Soon after, she filed for divorce.

Shortly after Mamie's divorce, Hugh Courtney came to work at the hotel and became good friends with the Moores, especially Mamie. He and Mamie started courting and married on November 10, 1910. She and Hugh and the two children moved to the Chelan area, finding work and housing at several different farms. Hugh treated the children as his own, with love and caring. Harwood started school at Chelan Falls and continued his education in the Chelan area until 1917, when the family moved to Stehekin where he went to the old school at McGregor Flats for one term, finishing up the seventh grade. In March 1918, he moved back to Chelan with the Felix Tester family to continue his education and work part-time for board and room, but that part-time work turned into a full-time job taking care of and milking ten cows as well as other farm chores. Soon, his grades began to drop, and the teacher decided he should take part of the seventh grade over again. Upon hearing that, Hugh decided Harwood should come back home and help out on their newly-acquired homestead. He could go to school in Stehekin and help with the many chores on the ranch, but he needed to work in Chelan for a week at a paying job just to get enough money for the boat fare to come home. Hugh and Mamie were flat broke, and a letter from Mamie in part spells it out pretty well:

"…. We got moved yesterday and are pretty well mixed up this morning but it is going to be fine and we all like it. I am sure you will too. I am sorry that you can't make your grade this time. It's too bad he put you so far back but maybe he knows what he's doing. Papa thinks that as long as you can't make your grade this spring that you had better work a week and then come home and go to school here this summer. I am so afraid you will get sick down there. Now dear, be sure and find a good place to work for that week. Be sure and don't lift too hard and don't let them work you to pieces and don't go where there is any sickness. We are clear out of money so can't send you any to come home on. Must stop now and get Papa some lunch, as he has to go to the boat this afternoon.

With lots of love from all, your loving mother,
Mamie Courtney."

Harwood came back home to go to school with Dorothy for the summer session and help out at the homestead. However, the urge to travel and see new places pulled at Harwood, and by the middle of November 1918, he found himself living on a ranch at Naches, Washington. Mamie was finding that keeping Harwood, barely fourteen years old, in one place was becoming a challenge. Getting a job and earning money turned out to be much more attractive to

Harwood about 1920.

him than sitting in a classroom all day. For many young men from struggling families, it was more necessity, than choice, to leave school and contribute to the meager family income.

After working in Naches most of the winter, Harwood was offered a job back in Stehekin for O.P. Maxwell, digging irrigation ditches for his hayfields. At least two ditches— one from Coon Run to the main field, and another from the river, for the field between the house and the river— had to be dug. The upper ditch, from Coon Run, was at least a half-mile in length— an enormous task alone. The lower one was not much shorter and just as much of a challenge. In those days, all of the work was done by hand, dynamite, and horses. Ditching with dynamite works well in certain soils, but in heavier, rocky ground, more powder is needed in holes closer together— about two feet apart in a line along the route of the ditch. It is unclear whether Mac or someone else taught Harwood the use of blasting powder, but it turned out to be a skill he used later in life when he worked in the mines.

Harwood continued living in Stehekin most of the time over the next several years, working for anyone who had a job for him. He liked to gamble and enjoyed frequent trips to town sitting in on the games at local card rooms in Chelan and Wenatchee. Most often his winnings were few, but as most gamblers addicted to the cards, he always said, "It's just a matter of time until you hit the big one." On paydays, the sky was the limit, but usually by the end of the weekend, he came home broke and tired, at times borrowing a few dollars from sympathetic friends and relatives to get him through until the next payday. Hugh and Mamie frowned on that lifestyle but always welcomed him in their home, even though it was agonizing to see him go to town and spend his hard-earned money so freely.

In early 1928, Harwood came home with a woman named Ruth. Turns out they had recently married after a very brief courtship. Mamie, reminiscing to my mother, recalled how Ruth never left the cabin the whole time they were there. The deep snow and cold weather apparently didn't appeal to her, and soon she and Harwood were on the boat heading back to town. Predictably, that marriage was short-lived. Actually, it went on for five years, but she left him almost six months, to the day, after they married.

Harwood went to work for Howe Sound Mining Company at Holden, Washington in 1930, helping develop the infrastructure and tunnels for the new underground copper mine. Holden was a developing mining town, named after an early pioneer, James Holden, who discovered the ore body in the late 1800s. The mine is located forty miles up Lake Chelan and twelve miles west of the lake at an elevation

Construction of the concentrate mill at Holden, Washington about 1936.

1500-foot level at the Holden Mine showing tracks between the portal and car dumping station.

The Holden concentrate mill in winter with Bonanza Mountain in background.

of 3200 feet. It lies deep in the heart of the North Cascades Mountains, and at the time of discovery, the only access was by boat and pack animals. The challenges of developing a mine in such a rugged, remote part of the country were numerous. Many said it couldn't be done, and in the early days, they may have been right. By the time Howe Sound Mining Company became involved in the late 1920s, however, they had the technology, capital and perseverance to make it happen. Management had many obstacles to overcome to get the mine up and running and into full production. Milling the ore, getting power to the mine, a town site location, pollution and transportation were just a few of the challenges facing the company. Even with the depression in full swing and the production schedule target date pushed back, the company kept quite a few men working at the mine. Men of Swedish, Norwegian, Russian, Canadian, Lithuanian, Danish and Finish origin worked alongside Harwood in the mine.

While visiting friends in Oregon in 1933, Harwood met Hazel McKamey in Hood River, later getting married on May 5, 1934. Hazel had two children, Peggy and Inez, from a previous marriage. The girls stayed in Oregon with their father when Hazel and Harwood went back to Chelan. Inez, the youngest, spent some time with her mother in Washington, but it is unclear just how much. I remember meeting her a few times when I was still living at home in the early1950s, but she was older and married by then. I don't recall ever meeting Peggy.

When the mine went into production in 1937, Harwood continued working, mostly underground in various jobs such as blasters helper, drill operator and mucker (the guys who actually loaded the ore carts.) Hazel and Inez lived with Hugh and Mamie in Stehekin part of the time, and in Chelan and Wenatchee while Harwood worked at the mine.

Living in a company town was a bit different than living elsewhere. Holden had its own currency…tin fifty-cent pieces, to supplement the federal currency system, mostly because of the lack of a bank. When employees and their families wanted money, they signed receipts at the commissary; the payroll office then deducted that amount from the wages. Average wages in the late 1930s were about $5.00 per day, depending on the job you had. Laborers working outside received about $.75 a day less than the miners working underground, and $1.20 a day was deducted for board and room. The company didn't allow a liquor store in the settlement, hoping to keep a more alert work force. Men could, however, order alcohol through the bus driver; he was going to Lucerne on a regular basis, where there was a tavern and contact with the boat and barge crews who could pick up their spirits in Chelan. Some of the men also made home brew.

The population at Holden during the production years of 1938 –1957 stayed right around 600 people, 400 of whom were employed at the mine. During World War II, the demand for copper increased, and Holden Mine was an important supplier of that mineral. Because Holden Mine was considered a defense contractor, men working there were exempt from the military draft. Labor shortages occurred, however, and slow-downs took place when the mine reduced production while performing maintenance, drilling new tunnels, and doing safety work underground. The nineteen years of production produced the following amounts of minerals: 212 million pounds of copper, 600 ounces of gold, 40 million pounds of zinc and 2 million ounces of silver. Ten million tons of ore were brought out of the mountain through one portal to the concentrate mill to get the above quantities.

About 100 homes made up the family housing village of Winston, just up-valley from the center of town.

The tailings dump at Holden Mine.

The scales crew weighed the filled concentrate buckets before being hauled to the barges eleven miles away.

The crane used for loading and unloading Holden ore barges at Lucerne, Washington.

The side-dump ore cars on the way to the grizzly bars at the mill.

On March 8, 1942, daughter Nedra was born to Hazel and Harwood in Wenatchee. Sometime after the war in about 1946, Harwood left the mine and settled in Wenatchee with Hazel and Nedra. Over the next two or three years, he worked at several jobs, including Horseshoe Basin and other work in the Stehekin area. In 1949, Harwood went to work for Wells and Wade Hardware in Wenatchee as a truck driver, hauling orchard supplies and other building materials on the Coulee Dam route which included all the small towns and orchards along the way. He also acquired a small mine on the East side of the Columbia River between Orondo and East Wenatchee, following that elusive vein of rich ore he hoped would someday make him wealthy (not unlike the passion that kept him at the card tables). He occasionally recruited my dad to help him out when his compressor quit running, or for other mechanical and physical help.

After working for Wells and Wade about fifteen years, Harwood's job ended on a sour note. He was starting to wear down, and hard work was getting difficult. The driving part of the job was okay, but drivers had to load and unload their own trucks, work he couldn't do very well anymore. As a result, coffee breaks along the way became increasingly longer, causing him to get back to Wenatchee much later than necessary. Before long, management figured out what was going on and had to let him go. It was sad to see his working career end that way, but the cold, hard reality of age and a broken-down body doesn't get much sympathy from the guy writing the paycheck.

Harwood continued puttering at the mine, but with just his Teamsters Union retirement—he was still too young to draw Social Security—gas and other needed supplies simply weren't affordable.

In 1966, he and Hazel both turned sixty-two and started drawing reduced Social Security retirement, helping out considerably; but without any savings, they had to watch every cent. Harwood and Hazel settled into a simple existence of frugal spending. After Nedra married and moved away, they moved into a smaller, more affordable house on Maple Street in Wenatchee. Laurence, my mother and others stopped by frequently to take them to town and help out any way they could, and, when his Buick was running, Harwood visited them. He liked the company and reminiscing about the old days. In the winter of 1967-'68, Harwood was diagnosed with lung cancer. After that, his health declined pretty fast, though he hung on for about a year. On December 4, 1968, at sixty-four years old, Harwood passed away in a Wenatchee hospital. Ironically, he was the same age as his mother, Mamie, when she died in 1950.

Family picnic in Wenatchee including from left to right: Lona Courtney, June Barnhart, Hazel Lotspiech, Hilda Byrd, Robert Byrd, Dorothy Lotspiech Byrd, Christina Byrd in front, Maria Byrd, Harwood Lotspiech, Annette Byrd, Kenny Barnhart holding Marvin Courtney, and Kathleen Byrd, about 1960.

Part II ~ Chapter VI

Dorothy Lotspiech
1905 ~ 1984

On Thanksgiving Day, 1962, I was changing the engine on an old car parked out in front of the Avery house, just upriver from my grandparents' homestead cabin. A typical late fall day, it was cold and raining. I spread an old tarp over the A-frame, set up for the hoist, to help stay dry underneath, but it was a dark, wet, dismal day, and no matter how hard you tried, you still got wet.

My cousin, Bob Byrd, and his family, along with Bob's mother, Dorothy (visiting from Wenatchee), were living in the Avery place and getting ready to have Thanksgiving dinner. They invited me in, but it was starting to get dark, and I really needed to finish the job that day. In those days, without electricity, I didn't have the luxury of setting up a drop light under my so-called tent. I declined the offer, explaining my predicament, and kept on working. About an hour later, to my surprise, here comes Dorothy with a large plate of turkey dinner for me, and another, smaller plate with her dessert. Not only was she bringing me food, but she stayed out there in the half-dark, dripping tent to finish her meal with me. By then I had set up a kerosene Aladdin lamp to provide a little light. While we ate, Dorothy asked about the different engine parts and displayed a genuine interest in what I was doing. Always thinking of others and putting their needs above her own, that Thanksgiving Day so many years ago was characteristic of Dorothy's aspiration to make the world just a little better place to live. It may not have been the most comfortable Thanksgiving Day, but certainly was one of my most memorable.

As a child, it took me a long time to figure out why my mother and Dorothy were half-sisters. For some reason, it just didn't register that Grandma Courtney was married once before marrying Hugh. As far as I was concerned, they were always Grandma and Grandpa Courtney, period. As I got older and started to learn more about our family history, I realized Mamie had an earlier marriage to William Felix Lotspiech and Dorothy and Harwood were the two children from that marriage. Since Dorothy married Charlie Byrd in 1924, I never knew she was a Lotspiech. The only name I ever knew was Dorothy Byrd.

Dorothy and her mother Mamie Courtney sharing a laugh at the homestead. ca. 1919

Dorothy Lotspiech, born December 27, 1905 at Moore, Washington was mostly raised at the Moore Hotel until 1911, when her mother, Mamie, and second husband, Hugh Courtney, sold the property and moved to Chelan. (Refer to Chapter V for details on Mamie's first marriage.) Living in the Chelan area for a few years, the family then moved to Stehekin, where Hugh and Mamie filed on the abandoned William McComb homestead and took up residence in early 1918. The year prior to that, when Hugh and Mamie were living at the Lesh property in Stehekin, where Hugh was working in Frank Leshe's sawmill, Dorothy helped Mamie and Mrs. Lesh prepare meals for the crew working at the mill. There, she began to learn a skill that served her well the rest of her life. She loved working in the kitchen making hot cross buns, and her favorite— chicken and dumplings. Dorothy wanted to attend high school in Chelan and did so for several months, but Hugh and Mamie simply couldn't afford to support her in town, and she had to move home. Her education didn't stop there, though. She learned to sew and make quilts, while Hugh and the boys taught her carpentry and other responsibilities on the farm. Dorothy knew she would need to know as much as possible in order to raise a family during hard times, which turned out to be mostly on her own. A letter to Harwood at school in Chelan from Dorothy, dated March 11, 1918, describes life at the Lesh Sawmill:

"Dear Harwood,
Well I suppose you are getting up early in the morning and going to bed early at night. But early to bed and early to rise makes a man healthy, wealthy and wise you know. How many cows have Testers got? I suppose about ten. Have they any pigs that you have to feed? And little calves or chickens?

My thumb is nearly well now, but I fell down stairs today and nearly broke my neck. Ha. Ha. But I really did hurt my back and skinned my leg and arm. The funny part about it was Mamma was upstairs so we had to call Papa to lift the ladder up because I thought my back was broken for a minute and the ladder went thru a window. I nearly fainted. Betty (the cow) is going to lay out tonight. Guess Papa looked all over for her but couldn't find her.

Say Harwood, last night about midnight Mama heard Teddy (the dog) making an awful noise and then she heard something holler and then began to mew and then stopped and after awhile it began to holler again. Papa went to look for his tracks but couldn't see them and another man Mr. Lesh got by the name of Mr. Moore heard it too. We think it's a cougar.

Mr. Washburn is having a dickens of a time getting things fixed up. He hasn't got a pan or anything to do with. Mrs. Colwell baked some pies and cakes for the straw boss. They even make Howard get wood on Sunday and when he said he'd have to play awhile first, he went down to the logs and fell in, then they all made fun of him for going down there. I think it's a shame.

Mrs. Lesh says it's going to take an awful lot of things for the bunkhouse. Dear, we made some hot cross buns and they are certainly good. If the envelope was big enough I'd send you some. Remember, if you find any new songs to copy them down in your notebook.

Mr. Lesh expects six men Tuesday. I bet he don't get them. Mr. Washburn only has two men besides himself. He must have an awful lot to do. Ha. Ha.

When I fell downstairs, Mrs. Lesh even came to see what the matter was. Mr. Lesh told her that Mama was upstairs and Laurence and I took the ladder down. Ha. Ha.

I wish you were here now. We have a feast on I can't say what because it is against the law. You will have a good idea.

Well, I must close. I think I've said enough, don't you?
Dorothy Courtney or D.M.C. Crochet Cotton.
X means kisses. XXXXXXXXXXXXXXXX
O means hugs. OOOOOOOOOOOOOOOO"

(Even though, as a youngster, Dorothy chose to go by the name Courtney, Hugh never legally adopted her and Harwood.)

Charley Byrd, a man living in Stehekin and working for the U.S. Forest Service, started seeing Dorothy in the early 1920s. Seventeen years older, Charley knew a lot about farming and working in the woods. Dorothy had a deep infatuation for him and on July 4, 1924, despite her parents' adamant disapproval, Dorothy and Charley were married.

A couple of years prior to their marriage, Charley had acquired the old Igo Inlo homestead, located between the Stehekin River and the present-day state emergency airstrip. Actually, Oscar Hart filed before Charley, and at one point in time, they agreed to take the 117-acre homestead together. With disagreements about who would get what part and the Homestead Act giving veterans (Charley served in France in WWI) extra points, a reluctant community council arbitrating the dispute had to vote in favor of Charley getting the entire homestead. Oscar was a well-liked, good man, but Charley had the trump card.

Dorothy Lotspiech Byrd at the Byrd homestead.

Charley and Dorothy settled on the homestead and on May 8, 1925, their first child, Robert Lee, was born. An interesting note about ages and dates is that, born in 1888, Charley was only a year younger than Dorothy's stepfather, Hugh. Robert was only five years younger than his uncle, Ray Courtney.

For most men in the valley, the U.S. Forest Service provided jobs working on trails and manning the numerous fire lookouts around the valley, as well as bridge building, packing supplies into crews with horses and mules, firefighting and stringing phone lines to the lookout towers. Juggling chores on the homestead and working for the Forest Service kept Charley busy trying to make ends meet. The trail crews packed in to their camps on Sunday afternoons and didn't return until either Friday nights after work or early Saturday mornings. That didn't leave much time for domestic work and relaxing. Hugh and Mamie, and the older boys helped Dorothy when they could. Many trips were made by foot or horseback the two-and-a-half miles between the homesteads. In her journal, my mother wrote often of family members walking down to Dorothy's to help out, occasionally spending the night. In the early days, before Byrd's bridge was built across the river near their ranch, Charley and Dorothy had to make the trek up the trail to the Lesh place and cross the river there to go to the landing. When the water was low in the late summer and through the winter, they forded the river near their home with a wagon or on horseback thereby saving the extra two miles. After the bridge was built, the families got together and carved out a rough wagon road between the Lesh place and Byrds', making travel a little easier between the Courtney and Byrd homes. Before a bridge crossed Company Creek, fording that stream also became an issue. However, about two hundred yards northeast of the present-day powerhouse, the creek spreads out, and suitable crossings were achieved several months of the

year. After Laurence bought the first family car in 1927, Mamie and my mother frequently got a ride to Dorothy's when Curt and the others were going to get the mail, getting a ride home on the return trip.

On October 16, 1926, Dorothy gave birth to their second child, a girl they named Effie. Three years later, on July 18, 1929, daughter Jean was born. By that time, my mother was old enough to babysit, taking some of the workload off Dorothy. Excerpts from a few of June's journal entries indicate how much the Courtneys all helped out at Dorothy's:

The Byrd bridge (old swayback) just downriver from the present day Harlequin Bridge.

Courtney and Byrd families next to the Courtney cabin and the newly dug well.
Back row: Ray (pulling June's hair), Robert Byrd, and Curt Courtney. Middle row: June Courtney, Effie Byrd, Hugh and Mamie Courtney.
Front row: Jean Byrd.

"Friday, August 10, 1934
Weather: Clear and hot.
Mama and Dorothy helped with the work and visited this morning.
This afternoon they visited until a little after three, then Dorothy and
the kids went home. Ray and Robert went down and did Dorothy's
chores. They got home at noon. After dinner they went up to fix the
ditch and fooled around. I did the general housework this morning. I
washed Effie's and Jean's hair, ironed and did a little bit of everything
this afternoon. Laurence and Dad got home tonight at nine thirty."

"Sunday, August 19, 1934
Weather: Clear and hot
We all did up the general work this morning and about twelve thirty
we went down to Stehekin to take Dad to the boat. We left down
there when the boat left and went from there up to Bridge Creek. We
got back down to Dorothy's at five thirty. We ate supper there and
Mama and Curtice did her chores. After supper we went home and
Dorothy and the kids came up with us to stay overnight."

"Friday, August 31, 1934
Weather: Clear and hot.
Mama canned peaches all day. Curtice and Ray went down to
Rainbow Lodge to telephone this morning. They stopped on the way
back to pick some strawberries at Dorothy's. They brought Dorothy
and the kids up with them when they came. Dorothy talked to Mama
all afternoon. About five thirty Curtice went down to Stehekin to get
Dad. Dorothy and I rode down as far as her place and I stayed there
until Curtice and Dad came back."

When Robert reached high school age, Dorothy and Charley, along with the three children, moved to Wenatchee. Charley eventually got a job as a fireman in another part of the state, and once again,

Dorothy and the children were alone a lot of the time. She and Charley did, however, manage to buy a little farm in Monitor, a few miles west of Wenatchee. They had a large house and barn that allowed them to have cows, hogs, chickens and turkeys. Dorothy was always a hard-working person; to make ends meet, she closed off part of the house, turning it into a smaller unit to rent out. She sold dairy products and baked pies and other pastries. She and the children also worked seasonally in the orchards. They lived there until Robert graduated from Wenatchee High School.

Dorothy with her three children, Effie, Jean and Robert.
ca. 1937

Dorothy, standing at the far right of her graduating class at the School of Nursing, Oklahoma City, OK.

That year, Dorothy and Charley decided to sell the homestead to Art Peterson of Manson to help provide funding to move to Portland, Oregon where she and the children could attend Multnomah Bible College.

They also sold the Monitor property and that summer, packed up their belongings and moved to Portland. Charley was transferred to Tinker Air Force Base in Oklahoma City where he continued to work as a civilian fireman for the Air Force. In Portland, Dorothy managed an apartment house and cooked at the Bible College to provide extra income. When Effie graduated from Bible school, Jeannie and Dorothy moved to Oklahoma City where Charley had purchased a house in the suburb of Britton. Robert married Hilda Scott, a girl he met at school, and they moved to California for him to continue his education. Effie stayed in the Northwest doing missionary work until moving to South Africa, where she met and married Leonard Baillie, also a missionary from Salisbury.

In the early 1950s, after an increasingly complicated and difficult marriage, Dorothy and Charley divorced in Oklahoma City.

After that, Dorothy found a beautiful, three-story home with full basement that she turned into a Christian boarding house for young women, eventually providing housing for twenty. Being the hard-working, frugal person she was, Dorothy did all the cooking and care of the house. Before long, she was managing two or three more of these homes. She also took nurses' training and received her LPN license. In her spare time, she took swimming lessons and learned to play the piano.

About 1960, Dorothy moved back to the West Coast, settling for a short time in Northeast Oregon where Robert and his family were living, then moving on to Wenatchee where she went to work as a nurse at the Deaconess Hospital. After retiring from work in late 1963, Dorothy took a trip to visit Len and Effie in South Africa. That trip was cut short when she got word that Hugh had lung cancer and wasn't expected to live long. After his death in March 1964, she moved to Stehekin to work part-time babysitting for Ray and Esther, sewing in Curt's new upholstery shop, and helping Robert and his family, who had recently also moved to Stehekin.

The Byrd family. Standing in back: Effie, Robert, Hilda (Roberts wife) holding Annette, and Jean.
Front row: Kathleen, Charley, Dorothy, and Maria.

Dorothy with granddaughters, Annette, Maria and Kathleen.

Charley and Dorothy Byrd.

June Courtney Barnhart, Jean Byrd Ogden, Dorothy Lotspiech Byrd, Wenatchee, about 1967.

Dorothy continued to divide her time between Wenatchee and Stehekin in the early 1970s. When Robert and his family successfully bid on and won the National Park Service concession contract of the North Cascades Lodge in Stehekin, Dorothy managed the gift shop and did other odd jobs at the lodge, always helping out where needed. When Robert and Hilda's five-year contract at the lodge ended, they left Stehekin and took up residence in Entiat, Washington, a small town halfway between Wenatchee and Chelan. Dorothy moved back to Wenatchee, but in time grew lonesome for her son, Robert, and Stehekin. She started spending several days at a time living at their home in Entiat, eventually letting her apartment go and moving in with them. I think being physically closer to Stehekin, and the Christian life that Robert and Hilda were so devoted to, helped suppress those empty feelings of loneliness. Dorothy's health was also failing, and she needed someone with her nearly all of the time. When Robert suffered a heart attack in the spring of 1982 and was hospitalized for several days in Wenatchee, Hilda knew she'd have her hands full taking care of Robert when he returned home. Sadly, Hilda and Dorothy's siblings made the tough decision to move Dorothy to Parkside Convalescent center in Wenatchee, where she could receive the needed care, making it easier for June and Laurence to help run errands and do other chores for her. Dorothy's condition worsened over time, and after nearly three years at Parkside, she passed away on December 9, 1984, just a few days short of turning seventy-nine.

I think Dorothy's granddaughter, Maria Byrd Vodden said it well: *"Dorothy was a lovely, committed, Christian lady, very intelligent, hard-working, and creative. She was always giving of herself, helping others and her family."*

Dorothy Lotspiech Byrd at Lake Chelan, 1965.

Dorothy sewing bus cushions for her brother Curt.

PART III

OUR FAMILY TODAY

Upper Lake Chelan and the Stehekin Valley. Photo by Mike Barnhart.

Of the original fifty-three acres homesteaded by my grandparents, only about fifteen remain in the family, the bulk of the rest were sold to the federal government in the 1970s. Other mostly small lots were sold to private parties over the years prior to that. Sadly, the only building left on the homestead from the old days—the original cabin where my mother was born—was part of the acreage sold to the National Park Service. My cousin, Cliff, moved the small cabin of Ray's to the Stehekin Valley Ranch prior to the sale. Another small, eight-by-ten cabin built by Hugh for a lapidary shop in the 1950s, was sold and moved after he died in 1964. Later, I acquired the cabin , and moved it up Company Creek road to our place.

Today, twenty-five members of our family still live in the valley, fourteen of us on the homestead. My sister and five other cousins are scattered around in various places around the country. The two living grandchildren of Mamie and her first husband, William Lotspiech, live in the Midwest, with great-grandchildren and great-great-grandchildren living both there and closer to Lake Chelan and Stehekin.

Stehekin has changed since Hugh and Mamie first settled here in 1918. Life got considerably easier with the coming of better roads and vehicles, electricity and satellite Internet. What hasn't changed, however, is how we feel about this valley and our heritage. While progress, like time, can't be stopped—and we're all part of it—family traditions and lifestyles can be preserved. That happens in many ways here, and to some extent, other valley residents have chosen similar lifestyles. Most everyone heats with woodstoves, some still cook on wood ranges, and a few heat water with a copper coil in the stove or wrapped around the stovepipe.

Others live off -the-grid, having installed solar panels and small hydroelectric turbines to provide electricity for lights, refrigerators and even heating water to cut down on or eliminate the use of fossil fuels.

In these days of mobility and shifting populations, where most everyone is from someplace else, I am in awe that six generations of our family have lived at this end of the lake, five of them here in the Stehekin Valley on this homestead (four generations have attented the Stehekin School.) When you have roots that go back that far, it's easy to develop a sense of belonging; of pride and caring, not only for the land we live on, but for the entire valley and even the mountains around it. You get to know this place so intimately; like the trails into the high country that our grandfather helped survey and build; or the fertile ground where Mamie raised vegetables; or special, private places in the woods where our ancestors used to go—old trapping cabins and fishing holes; long forgotten camp sites like Bear Trap Springs, Wood Rat, or Cedar Camp. Walking around the homestead, I still find old oil cans or a rusting can of nuts and bolts sitting on a fir stump left from Granddad's sawmilling days.

After Grandmother died in 1950, the barn stood empty, with only the aroma of old logs, leather harnesses and cow manure to remind one of days long passed. It, too, was just another place to store things. The old milking stalls were still there— a tuft of cow hair stuck in the sliver of a board —along with the hoof-worn floorboards. Down the center, a couple piles of white pine and Alaskan cedar lumber waited to be transformed into kitchen cabinets for the "new house".

In the early 1970s, before Curt sold the remaining homestead to the National Park Service, he tore down the old barn and shack and burned them on the spot. They were in bad disrepair and becoming a safety hazard to folks wandering around the property. Later, when the government started using the new house for employee housing, a wiring short caused a fire and the house burned to the ground in about fifteen minutes.

Today, as my wife and I take our frequent walks down the road past the old place, my thoughts are flooded with memories of why this place means so much to me. Often, I stop to take a complete look around to bring it all back. The log and rough-lumber buildings all re-appear. I see the faces and activities of the homestead—Granddad sitting on a stump rolling a cigarette, Mom waking a grumbling Ray up from an afternoon nap just so she could take his picture with a couple of twin calves, Curt and Ray home on leave from World War II in their Army uniforms, posing for pictures by one of the big trees. It's all there, stories and memories I will always hold close.

Beans sitting on the trail to the old barn, waiting for Curt to come home from work. Photo by June Courtney Barnhart.

Ray with twin calves. Photo by June Courtney Barnhart.

Ray and Curt home on leave from World War II. ca.1942. Photo by June Courtney Barnhart.

Stehekin community photo 2008. Photo by Mike Barnhart.

Old homestead cabin 1986. Photo by Mike Barnhart.

Biography

Mike Barnhart on Boulder Butte.

Mike Barnhart was born in Wenatchee, Washington in 1944. At the age of fourteen, he started working for his uncle, Ray Courtney in Stehekin packing tourist groups into the high country of the North Cascades, while going to school in Wenatchee during the winter months. By 1960, Mikes love of the mountains and the Stehekin lifestyle began to pull him farther away from the city, and soon he was building a cabin on his grandparents homestead.

Early on, Mike became interested in photography and documenting life in Stehekin, while shooting with an old Brownie 620 box camera. Assigned to a helicopter company for two years with the Army in Vietnam, Mike continued taking pictures from the air and on the ground of village life and the Montagnard people near the Cambodian border.

After returning to Stehekin, Mike worked at a number of jobs in the valley, including nearly twenty years operating the small hydroelectric plant for Chelan County PUD, as well as forming Barnhart Photography with his wife Nancy. Over the years, Mike has shown his work throughout North Central Washington including several one-man shows, focusing on lifestyles of Stehekin and Vietnam. Barnhart Photography markets art prints, cards and books of their work.

Mike and Nancy continue to live in Stehekin. Mike has two adult children from a previous marriage, along with eight grandchildren; he and Nancy have two adult sons and one grandchild.